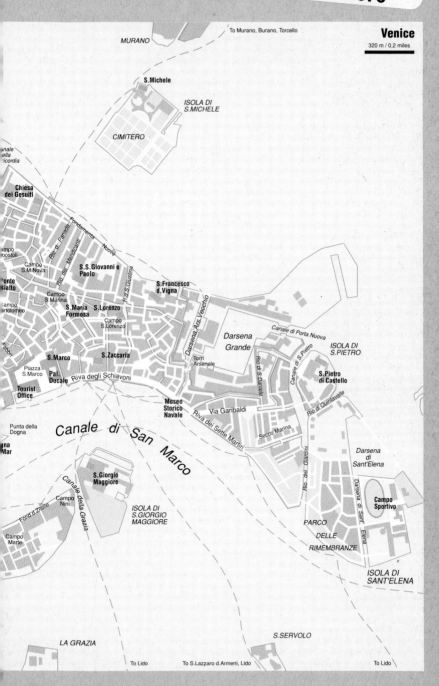

Venice

320 m / 0,2 miles

To Murano, Burano, Torcello

MURANO

S.Michele

ISOLA DI
S.MICHELE

CIMITERO

nale
ella
icordia

Chiesa
dei Gesuiti

Fondamenta
Rio dei Mendicanti
Rio d. Panada
Nuove

ampo
ostoli

Campo
S.M Nova

S.S.Giovanni e
Paolo

onte
ialto

Campo
S Marina

Rio di S.Giustina

S.Francesco
d.Vigna

ampo
artolomeo

S.Maria
Formosa

S.Lorenzo

Campo
S.Lorenzo

Darsena Ars.Vecchio

Darsena
Grande

Canale di Porta Nuova

ISOLA DI
S.PIETRO

Elbon

S.Marco

S.Zaccaria

Torri
Arsenale

Rio di S.Daniele

Canale di S.Pietro

S.Pietro
di Castello

Piazza
S.Marco

Pal.
Ducale

Riva degli Schiavoni

Tourist
Office

Punta della
Dogna

Rio di Quintavalle

na
Mar

Canale di San Marco

Museo
Storico
Navale

Via Garibaldi

Riva dei Sette Martiri

Secco Marina

Darsena
di
Sant'Elena

S.Giorgio
Maggiore

Canale della Grazia

Rio dei Giardini

Darsena di Sant' Elena

Campo
Nini

ISOLA DI
S.GIORGIO
MAGGIORE

Campo
Sportivo

Fond.d'Zitelle

Campo
Marte

PARCO
DELLE
RIMEMBRANZE

ISOLA DI
SANT'ELENA

LA GRAZIA

S.SERVOLO

To Lido

To S.Lazzaro d.Armeni, Lido

To Lido

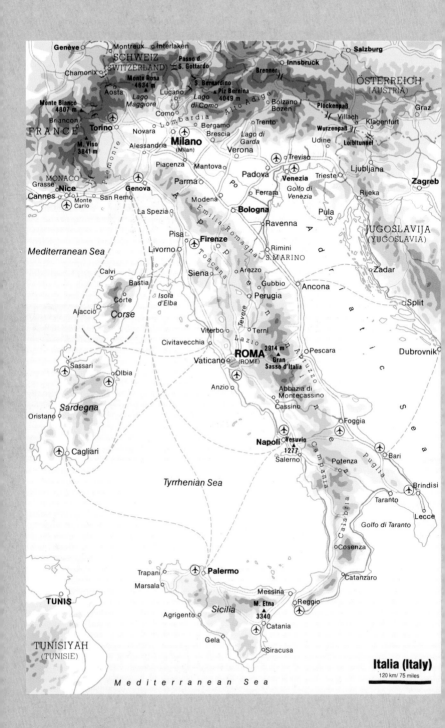

Italia (Italy)

120 km/ 75 miles

INSIGHT *pocket* GUIDES

Venice

Written and Presented by **Susie Boulton**

INSIGHT
pocket
GUIDES

Insight Pocket Guide:

Venice

Directed by
Hans Höfer

Editorial Director
Andrew Eames

Photography by
Chris Donaghue

Design Concept by
V. Barl

Design by
Gareth Walters

© **1993 APA Publications (HK) Ltd**

All Rights Reserved

Printed in Singapore by
Höfer Press (Pte) Ltd
Fax: 65-8616438

Distributed in the United States by
Houghton Mifflin Company
2 Park Street
Boston, Massachusetts 02108
ISBN: 0-395-65762-8

Distributed in Canada by
Thomas Allen & Son
390 Steelcase Road East
Markham, Ontario L3R 1G2
ISBN: 0-395-65762-8

Distributed in the UK & Ireland by
GeoCenter International UK Ltd
The Viables Center, Harrow Way
Basingstoke, Hampshire RG22 4BJ
ISBN: 9-62421-541-3

Worldwide distribution enquiries:
Höfer Communications Pte Ltd
38 Joo Koon Road
Singapore 2262
ISBN: 9-62421-541-3

Benvenuto!

Welcome! To a city which, more than any in the world, has captivated, enchanted and seduced. Not that it has always been love at first sight. I first saw Venice on a cold, wet April day 20 years ago. The lagoon was a steely grey and the waters of the Grand Canal lapped lugubriously against the crumbling fabric of its great *palazzi;* Italian school children filled the streets and squares with the cacophony of their ghettoblasters. This was not the Venice of Turner, Proust and Hemingway. Like D H Lawrence I began to see 'an abhorrent, green slippery city' and one which was rapidly grabbing my lire and giving little in return.

But, as the cliché says, 'to know Venice is to love Venice'. Through frequent visits to research and write about the city I came to the realisation that there was nowhere else to match her for sheer beauty and charm. More than any city I know, Venice invites digression. Wherever you look there is something to catch the eye: a vine spilling over a wrought-iron balcony, a glimpse of fresco through a half-open shutter, a bas-relief of a Madonna and Child high on a wall, a sleek black gondola gliding silently down a canal.

Bearing in mind that it is this wealth of incidental detail that makes Venice such an appealing place, I have constructed a series of leisurely itineraries designed to lead you first to the celebrated sights, then steer you deeper into Venice, away from the crowds, through some of my own favourite streeets and squares. And just in case the art and architecture become too much, I have included trips through the lagoon to the Lido and the outlying islands. My purpose is to show you the quintessential magic of Venice, so that when you step back into reality, where the houses are built on terra firma, it takes time and a tug to readjust. — Susie Boulton

Contents

Maps

HISTORY

From Swamps to Silks and Spices

The mudflats and swampy marshes of the Venetian lagoon held little allure for the barbarian marauders who swept into Italy in the 5th century AD. So the coastal dwellers, fleeing from the onslaught, sought sanctuary on the low-lying lagoon islands. The settlers were a sociable lot and by the 7th century had founded a kind of duchy ruled from Byzantium. By the beginning of the 9th century the seat of the duchy was the *Rivus Altus*, a group of islands named after a deep channel which divides them. These islands became known as the Rialto.

Detail from 'The State Barge of the Doge' by Canaletto

CULTURE

The Arab conquest of Egypt and the Levant had left the Byzantine Empire low on food supplies and it was Venetian merchants who filled the gap. The Rialto became a key trading centre where spices, silks and other luxuries of the East were exchanged for corn, salt, oil and other necessities from the West. This marked the beginning of Venice's vast commercial expansion and the foundation of her civilisation. Little by little, as her trade expanded, she threw off her Byzantine yoke. By the year 1000 the Orseolo dynasty ruled in the Rialto and the independent authority of Doge Pietro Orseolo II was recognised by Constantinople. In the late 11th century, in return for her help in repelling the Normans from Greece, Venice was granted trading preferences over other merchants. Venice had truly come of age.

Merchants created Venice's wealth

Power and Prosperity

During the 13th century Venice gained power by deft use of commerce and diplomacy. The most significant (though ignominious) event was the Fourth Crusade, whose destination was to be Egypt (centre of Muslim power in the Near East) but which ended in the destruction of the Christian Byzantine Empire. In return for payment and an equal division of the conquered territories, Venice agreed to provide the transport for the Crusade. She then waived payment for assistance by the crusaders in her reconquest of Zara, lost to Hungary in 1186. When Zara fell she then persuaded the Crusade, in the teeth of Papal opposition, to divert its mission to Constantinople, The Byzantine emperor was deposed, the city sacked and a *de facto* government established by the Venetians and

Removal of the bronze horses of San Marco

the crusaders. Huge quantities of booty went to Venice, including the famous bronze horses of San Marco.

By 1261 Venice enjoyed possession of a chain of ports and supply bases through Dalmatia to Constantinople and the Black Sea. Her acquisitions inevitably attracted the envy of commercial competitors – in particular Genoa which had also been granted trading privileges by Byzantium and which had her eye on a trading monopoly in the Eastern Mediterranean. This would involve the defeat of her bitter enemy, Venice. Sea battles ensued and the intense rivalry climaxed in the great war of Chioggia when the Genoese fleet entered the Venetian lagoon, captured and sank Venetian ships and blocked off escape routes. They seemed on the point of victory but, under Doge Andrea Contarini, Venice built a new fleet and barricaded the canals. Turning defence into attack, she besieged and finally defeated the Genoese navy at Chioggia in 1380. The war exhausted Genoa financially and marked the beginning of her naval decline.

Doge and Oligarchy

By the end of the 14th century Venice had developed a true republican constitution, full of checks and balances. The position of the doge had passed from one of supreme authority to that of a kind of elected constitutional monarch. In 1355 Doge Marin Falier had tried to hijack the growing power of Venice's governing bodies and was consequently executed for treason.

As the constitution developed so the doge's powers diminished. He was elected by an aristocratic oligarchy under a complex voting system and took a solemn promise not to exceed his powers. By the 15th century these were so curtailed that he was not permitted to leave Venice or speak to a foreign visitor in private. The weightiest decisions of state, such as the appointment of ministers and the declaration of war, were taken by the Great Council of 480 members nominated by the six *sestieri* – the official districts of Venice. The more wieldy Council of State, which grew from 60 to 300 members, made the everyday executive decisions. Smaller in size, yet vital for the security of the republic, was the Council of 10 – a cross between a court of law and Secret Service which sent traitors, such as the celebrated *condottiere*, Carmagnola, to the gallows.

Zenith and the Seeds of Decline

The 15th century saw the zenith of Venetian power. At the dawn of the century, in addition to her maritime empire, she was mistress of the greater part of the Veneto region north of Venice and was moving deeper into the mainland. Under the aggressive, western-orientated policy of Doge Francesco Foscari, she carried her dominions to Brescia and Bergamo and then to Ravenna and the River Adda. The extent of her power inevitably aroused bitter jealousy in Europe. The belligerent Pope Julius II, bent on reducing Venice's power to that of a fishing port, allied with the Holy Roman Empire, Spain, France, Naples, Milan and other Italian states. Venice temporarily lost many of her recent acquisitions but, perhaps worse, was subjected to public humiliation when her ambassadors were forced to kneel before the pope while the terms of her submission were declaimed.

A more permanent threat came from the east. In 1453, the Ottoman Turks had finally taken Constantinople, heralding the arrival of a new power in Europe. Venice sought to maintain her commercial pre-eminence in the east, mainly by diplomacy and appeasement, but at times was forced to confront the Turks. She lost key Greek and Albanian ports in the war of 1463–70 and the Peloponnese and parts of her Adriatic shores in that of 1499–1503. A third blow, at the turn of the 15th century, was the rounding of Africa by Vasco da Gama, establishing the Portuguese spice trade and stripping Venice of its virtual monopoly.

Palazzo ceiling by Tintoretto

Artistic Heyday

While the seeds of decline were sown abroad, on a cultural level Venice continued to prosper. Famous painters such as the Bellinis, Carpaccio, Giorgione, Titian, Tintoretto and Veronese gave new impact to Renaissance art by their original use of colour and light (see Itinerary 3 in the *Pick & Mix* section). The great patrons of art in Venice were the doge, the commercial aristocracy and the *scuole* – devotional and charitable organisations who decorated their buildings with lavish works by leading artists. Venice was seen as a

Gothic windows

major cultural centre and an increasing number of visitors came to see the artistic wonders of the city.

While the Renaissance flourished in Florence, the distinctive and unique Venetian Gothic was at its height in Venice, the masterpiece being the **Ca' d'Oro**. With the Renaissance came Mauro Coducci (who built the first Renaissance church in Venice), the Lombardi family, who produced some of the finest sculpture and churches of the city, and Sansovino, the architect of the Library, the Mint and the Loggetta. A little later came Palladio, an exponent of strict classical form and the most influential of all Italian architects. The only churches he built happen to be in Venice. San Giorgio Maggiore and the Redentore are unsurpassed in their cool rational, classical beauty.

Venetian Renaissance architecture has a very distinctive feel. Palladio excepted, it is as much about the rational use of a variety of architectural traditions as the consistent application of classical form. Another factor is the absence of fortification in its *palazzi*. Thirdly, the light, reflected in the waters of the city, tends to soften shadows, dematerialise form and thereby give a joyful lightness to the buildings.

San Giorgio Maggiore's classical beauty

Detail from Vincento's 'The Battle of Lepanto'

Fluctuating Fortunes

The 16th century witnessed the rise of the Hapsburg dynasty which, by the middle of the century, was ruling – directly or indirectly – in Milan, Naples, Sicily, Sardinia, Genoa and Florence. By her policy of watchful passivity Venice was able to retain her independence. In the east she tried to continue her policy of appeasement with the Turks but in 1570 the Sultan demanded the cherished island of Cyprus. When Venice refused, Nicosia was sacked and the island taken with terrible bloodshed. This prompted a brave reaction which was celebrated throughout Christendom.

In 1571 a Christian fleet, including many Venetian ships, won a great victory off Lepanto with the loss of 30,000 Turks and the destruction of hundreds of her galleys. Unhappily for Venice this did not mark the beginning of a sustained fight back and shortly afterwards Venice sued for peace and recognised the loss of Cyprus. Back home bubonic plague had reduced the population by about a third. Scarcely had Venice recovered from the effects of a further plague in 1630 when the Turkish army landed in Crete and Venice was forced to cede this important stronghold. Despite the military victories that followed, Venice was never to return to her former glory.

End of the Republic

During the 18th century Venice was in terminal political and commercial decline. Venetian life became hedonistic and decadent. The ruling classes abandoned themselves to leisure and luxury, frittering away the fortunes they had made during the republic's heyday. Life was a perpetual round of festivals and masked balls, music and gambling. This was the era of the notorious libertine, Casanova, and the great artist Tiepolo, whose illusionistic frescoes are suitably sensuous and carefree.

In 1789 Ludovico Manin, a weak, newly arrived aristocrat from the Friuli, was appointed doge. In 1796 Napoleonic troops crossed into northern Italy and took Venetian Verona. Napoleon offered the republic an alliance and, on her refusal, sent General Juno to the Rialto with an ultimatum. Some citizens called for resistance but most knew it was futile. The Great Council convened. The sound of a shot, believed by the councillors to have been fired by a revolutionary, but in fact fired by a friendly parting Dalmatian sailor, sent them scurrying to the ballot boxes. They voted overwhelmingly for surrender. Manin was the last doge and 1,000 years of La Serenissima had come to an end.

At the close of the Napoleonic wars, Venice, along with substantial parts of Italy, came under the almost universally hated rule of the Austrians. Soon Italian patriotism was spreading in the peninsula. The Venetians rose up against the Metternich government, forced the Austrians to withdraw and set up a new republic. The city was put under siege; five months of hunger, disease and bombs (dropped from balloons, the first air raid in history) forced Venice to surrender in August 1849; Austrian rule was reimposed. In 1861 the greater part of Italy was unified and, five years later, Venice became part of the new kingdom of Italy.

The City in the Sea – Venice in Peril

Geographically, Venice is unique. It is built on an archipelago of 118 islets, supported by billions of wooden stakes driven into the mud and linked by 400 bridges. The only link with *terra firma* is the Ponte della Libertà. It is the only city in the world which is built entirely on water – a factor which contributes not only to its splendour, but also to its gradual decay.

On 14 November 1966, Venice was flooded for 13 hours to a depth of nearly 2m (6ft 6in). A second flood soon followed. Under the umbrella of UNESCO, 30 or so private organisations went into action to save the city. The British Venice in Peril Fund has been a major contributor to the restoration of churches, monuments and mosaics and played a leading role in the successful campaign to prevent Expo 2000 from being sited in the Veneto.

But, despite all the efforts, there is never enough money to insure against the problems of pollution, ecology and potential flooding – all of which are a constant threat to the city's unique heritage. (Donations can be sent to: Venice in Peril Fund, 24 Rutland Gate, London SW7 1BB, United Kingdom; Tel: 071-823 9203)

As the cost of housing and restoration rises, so does the number of Venetians leaving for cheaper accommodation in Mestre. An increasing number of foreigners are moving in or buying an apartment as a *pied-à-terre*. And the Venetian population, now around 80,000, is down to half what it was in 1945 and to between a half and a third of what it used to be during the heyday of the Empire.

Historical Outline

5th–6th centuries AD Refugees fleeing from barbarians settle in the lagoon.

696 Election of the first doge, Paoluccio Anafesto.

828 Body of St Mark, stolen from Alexandria, is smuggled to Venice. St Marco replaces St Theodore as patron saint of Venice. San Marco church built to enshrine his body.

991–1008 Reign of Doge Pietro Orseolo II. Commercial advantages obtained from Byzantium and a great sea victory against the Dalmatians.

1044 Electoral system of doge formalised to prevent nepotism.

1082–5 Defeat of Sicilian Normans at sea.

1104 The Arsenale is founded.

1177 Venice hosts a great assembly reconciling the pope, Alexander III, and the Holy Roman Emperor, Frederick Barbarossa.

1202–4 Venice diverts the fourth Crusade, and enriches herself by the sack of Constantinople.

1256 Marco Polo born in Venice. He becomes the first European to visit China, bringing back amazing tales and the secret of making spaghetti (Italians deny this).

1310–14 Tiepolo and Querini plot to oust Doge Gradenigo.

1339 War with Verona under the della Scala family gains Treviso, Conegliano and Castelfranco.

1355 Doge Marin Falier beheaded for treason.

1380 War with Genoa ends in Venetian victory at Chioggia.

1405 Venice takes Verona from Milan.

1423 Election of Doge Francesco Foscari begins Venetian expansion to Bergamo and Brescia and on to parts of Cremona.

1453 Turks take Constantinople heralding the Ottoman empire in Europe.

1454 Peace of Lodi confirms Venetian gains in Italy.

1498 Vasco da Gama reaches the East Indies; begins the loss of Venice's spice monopoly.

1508 League of Cambrai against Venice results in territorial losses on land.

1571 Resounding victory against Turks at Lepanto.

1606 Inspired by Paulo Sarpi, Venice successfully defies a papal interdict.

1699 Reconquest of the Peloponnese by Venice.

1718 Venice ratifies return of the Peloponnese to the Turks under the Treaty of Passarowitz.

1797 Napoleonic troops enter Venice and the Republic ends.

1815 Treaty of Vienna puts the Veneto under Austrian control.

1848 Venice under Daniele Manin rebels against Austria and the city is put under siege.

1866 Venice becomes part of unified Italy after Prussians defeat Austrians at Sadowa.

1914–18 During World War I over 600 bombs are dropped on the city, but damage to monuments is not as great as was feared.

1920s and 1930s Construction of large commercial harbour and oil refinery at Marghera.

1966 Disastrous flooding leads to the launch of the International Appeal to save the city.

1973 Special law passed to reduce pollution of lagoon waters.

1987 A project is authorised for the building of giant sliding gates at the lagoon entrance to prevent flooding.

Day Itine...

One of the delights of Venice is that there are no motor cars. The streets and alleys are simply not wide enough. Anyone arriving by car must park in one of the car parks on the northern periphery of the city, either at Tronchetto (a parking island) or Fusina, at the mouth of the Breita Canal. In reality, garaging costs are so high that it is far better to reach the city by train or by air (see *Practical Information*).

To get about Venice, either walk or travel by the excellent waterbus network. Walking really is the best way to get to know the city. Venice is not big, but it is a warren of little alleys, bridges and canalside paths in which it is easy to get lost. Even people who know the city very well get lost from time to time only to emerge close to a familiar landmark. Losing your way is fun because you will discover quiet canals where life goes on untouched by the tourist bustle, and you will never be very far away from a main thoroughfare, marked with the ubiquitous yellow direction signs pointing to major landmarks, such as San Marco, the Rialto or Piazzale Roma.

For getting about by water, you have a choice, ranging from the reliable and inexpensive waterbus network, through metered water taxis which carry up to four passengers, to gondolas; the latter are the most expensive forms of transport, only to be used if you don't need to count the cost, or for those special romantic occasions (see *Nightlife* for a suggested gondola ride and *Practical Information* for other transport details).

Piazza San Marco

DAY 1

Oriental Extravaganza

Piazza San Marco, the focus of Venetian life, makes a fitting start and finish to your first day in the city. See inside the great Basilica di San Marco, take a trip on a 'vaporetto' to the island of San Giorgio and see it all in spectacular panorama. Visit the Doge's Palace, then spend the afternoon boating up the Grand Canal to admire the parade of 'palazzi'.

On your first visit to Piazza San Marco you will do well to take in no more than a fraction of its history, art and incomparable beauty.

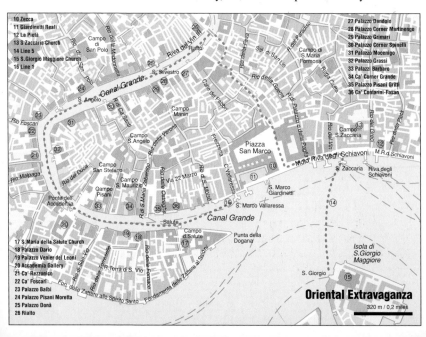

10 Zecca
11 Giardinetti Reali
12 La Pietà
13 S Zaccaria Church
14 Line 5
15 S.Giorgio Maggiore Church
16 Line 1

17 S.Maria della Salute Church
18 Palazzo Dario
19 Palazzo Venier dei Leoni
20 Accademia Gallery
21 Ca' Rezzonico
22 Ca' Foscari
23 Palazzo Balbi
24 Palazzo Pisani Moretta
25 Palazzo Donà
26 Rialto

27 Palazzo Dandolo
28 Palazzo Corner Martinengo
29 Palazzo Grimani
30 Palazzo Corner Spinelli
31 Palazzo Mocenigo
32 Palazzi Grassi
33 Palazzi Barbaro
34 Ca' Corner Grande
35 Palazzo Pisani Gritti
36 Ca' Contarini-Fasan

Oriental Extravaganza

320 m / 0,2 miles

Florian's coffee-house

Take things at a leisurely pace and come back for more another day. Your starting point is **Florian's**, prince of Venetian coffee-houses and ex-haunt of the *literati*. Splash out just this once and order coffee, following in the footsteps of a long line of illustrious clients, among them Byron, Dickens, Proust and Guardi. Linger as long as you like, preferably *al fresco,* to admire what is arguably the most beautiful, and certainly the most eulogised, square in the world. Napoleon called it the most elegant drawing room in Europe. One wonders why he then proceeded to hack down one end of it – the Ala Napoleonica to your left – in doing so destroying Sansovino's church of San Geminiano.

The square is the one and only *piazza* in Venice. What it lacks in harmony is compensated by the splendour of individual architectural features. The jewel in the crown is the **Basilica di San Marco**, shrine of the Republic and symbol of Venetian glory. The sumptuous exterior, bubbling with domes and encrusted with mosaics, marbles and carvings, has attracted comment from the censorious 'a barbaric building like a great Mongolian pleasure pavilion' (Jan Morris), to the affectionate 'a vast warty bug taking a meditative walk' (Mark Twain).

The nearby **Campanile** looks much as it did when it assumed its present form in the early 16th century. Which would not be surprising were it not for the fact that it collapsed in a heap on 14 July 1902. Amazingly the only casualty was the custodian's cat and

Basilica di San Marco from the Campanile

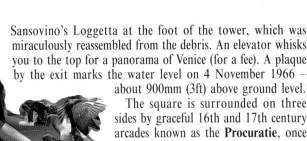

Sansovino's Loggetta at the foot of the tower, which was miraculously reassembled from the debris. An elevator whisks you to the top for a panorama of Venice (for a fee). A plaque by the exit marks the water level on 4 November 1966 – about 900mm (3ft) above ground level.

The square is surrounded on three sides by graceful 16th and 17th century arcades known as the **Procuratie**, once the lavish apartments of Venice's nine procurators or top-ranking officials.

Leave the café when the doors of the **Basilica** open at 9.30am and admire the façade close up. Expect to see at least part of it under scaffolding – seeing the building in its entirety is a rare event. The four horses over the central portal are replicas of the original team which were looted from Constantinople during the Fourth Crusade (1204) and which, to protect them from pollution and pigeon droppings, were removed to the inside of the building. Of the mosaics decorating the entrances and upper portals only the one above the door on the far left – *The Translation of the Body of the Saint to the Church of San Marco* – is original. Look closely to see how the Basilica looked in the 13th century. The far right lower portal has a mosaic showing how the body of St Mark was taken from Alexandria, reputedly smuggled under slices of pork. Turbaned Muslims are showing their revulsion at the smell – the one in the blue cloak is holding his nose.

For an overview of the entire Basilica the best place is the **Gallery** on the first floor. When it opens at 10am take the steep narrow steps off the narthex marked Loggia dei Cavalli which will bring you to the **Marciano museum**.

Interior of the basilica

On this level you can see more easily the myriad of mosaics (covering roughly one acre/4,000m^2) and the floor which looks like an oriental carpet. You can also go out on to the terrace and look down on the piazza just as doges and dignitaries used to do during processions and lavish celebrations.

On the ground level of the Basilica, single out the oldest and finest of the mosaics which are in the domes and date from the 12th and 13th centuries. The Pentecost Dome, the first as you go along the nave, was probably the earliest to be decorated. The central dome has another spectacular mosaic, whose theme is the *Ascension of Christ*, also dating from the late 12th or early 13th century.

21

The view from San Giorgio Maggiore

The greatest treasure of all is the **Pala d'Oro**, hiding behind the altar (enter through the St Clement Chapel on the right of the rood screen; open weekdays 10am–5pm, Sunday 1.30pm–5pm). This *pièce de resistance*, encrusted with pearls, sapphires, emeralds and enamels, was first commissioned for Doge Pietro Orseolo in the 9th century, then changed and enriched over the centuries. Despite Napoleon's pickings, there are still about 2,000 jewels. Yet more Byzantine loot is stored in the **Treasury** (entered from the right transept). The prize piece is the Pyx, an embossed silver-gilt casket in the shape of a Byzantine church.

There are many other splendid features in the Basilica, among them the chapels, the roodscreen and the Baptistry. But there is little satisfaction in trying to cover all the details in one visit. Already dazzled by Byzantine and Gothic splendour you will now probably appreciate a short jaunt across the water to the **island of San Giorgio Maggiore**, perhaps the most picturesque landmark of Venice. Walk left along the waterfront until you come to the S Zaccaria landing stage opposite the Savoia & Jolanda Hotel. Wait for a No 5 *vaporetto* marked *circolare destra*. The trip takes four minutes and the boat drops you off just below the church. Step inside the cool, classical interior, then follow the signs for the Campanile. A lift operated by one of the monks from the nearby monastery will take you up to the top for a breathtaking panorama of the city

The Palazzo Ducale

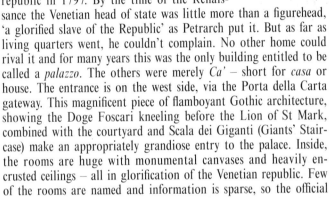

Relaxing outside the Palazzo Ducale

and surrounding area, stretching, on a good day, as far as the Alps. The church has three late works by Tintoretto: *The Last Supper* and *Gathering of the Manna* on the chancel walls and, hanging in the Chapel of the Dead, the *Deposition*.

The return trip affords splendid views of the San Marco waterfront, and particularly the florid Gothic façade of the **Palazzo Ducale** (Doge's Palace; April–October 8.30–7pm; November–March 9am–4pm). This was the home of the doges and seat of Venetian government from the 9th century to the fall of the republic in 1797. By the time of the Renaissance the Venetian head of state was little more than a figurehead, 'a glorified slave of the Republic' as Petrarch put it. But as far as living quarters went, he couldn't complain. No other home could rival it and for many years this was the only building entitled to be called a *palazzo*. The others were merely *Ca'* – short for *casa* or house. The entrance is on the west side, via the Porta della Carta gateway. This magnificent piece of flamboyant Gothic architecture, showing the Doge Foscari kneeling before the Lion of St Mark, combined with the courtyard and Scala dei Giganti (Giants' Staircase) make an appropriately grandiose entry to the palace. Inside, the rooms are huge with monumental canvases and heavily encrusted ceilings – all in glorification of the Venetian republic. Few of the rooms are named and information is sparse, so the official guide book is worth buying.

Ceiling in the Palazzo Ducale

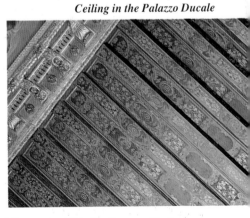

The gold and white stuccoed Scala d'Oro (Golden Staircase) takes you up to the doge's private apartments, only accessible to the public during special exhibitions, then up again to the council rooms. Outstanding among these are: the **Anticollegio**, the waiting room for ambassadors, decorated with works by Tintoretto and Veronese's *Rape of Europe* (opposite the window wall); the **Sala del Collegio**, where the Council of State met with the doge, with its superb ceiling and some magnificent works by Veronese, including *Justice and Peace Offering the Sword and Scales to Venice Enthroned*; the **Senate Room**, with another elaborate ceiling with paintings by Tintoretto and assistants; the **armoury** section; the **Sala del Consiglio dei Dieci**, where the Council of 10 (in fact about 30) tried crimes against the state, with ceiling paintings by Veronese; and –

grandest of all – the **Sala del Maggior Consiglio,** the huge Assembly Hall, where the doges were elected and where the last doge abdicated. The proportions are monumental – sufficient to accommodate 3,000 guests when Henry III of France was entertained here at a state banquet in 1574. The ceiling consists of panels painted by leading artists of the time, among them Tintoretto and Veronese whose *Apotheosis of Venice* stands out for its dramatic perspective. Tintoretto's massive *Paradise* covering the entire east wall was for

The Bridge of Sighs

a long time the biggest painting in the world: a staggering feat for a man of 70. Below the ceiling a frieze shows the first 76 doges. Note the blacked-out space which should belong to Marin Falier, the doge executed for treason in 1355.

From the splendour of the council rooms you are plunged, as were the prisoners, into the dungeons. The *pozzi*, the dungeons beneath the palace were dark, dank and infested with rats; the *piombi*, where Casanova entertained and masterminded his daring escape, were salubrious in comparison. The new prisons, which are those you see today, are reached via the **Bridge of Sighs** (where you can peep through the grills), named after the sighs of prisoners as they were led over the bridge to torture or execution – or so the story goes. In fact, by the time the bridge was built in the 17th century the cells, by European standards, were comparatively civilised and used only for petty offenders. Only one political prisoner ever crossed the bridge.

It is time now for lunch and a rest from sights. Being San Marco, whatever you choose will be expensive. For a range of prices try **Frezzeria**, west of the piazza. At the pricey end of the market is **La Colomba**, **Piscina di Frezzeria**, well known for fish, fashionable clientele and 20th-century paintings. Mid-range is **Città di Vittorio**, signposted off Frezzeria, popular with Venetians for simple cooking. **Le Chat qui Rit,** at the top end of the street, is a popular self service bar with good sandwiches and snacks.

The afternoon will be spent on a leisurely boat ride up the **Grand Canal**. Your means of travel will be the No 1 *vaporetto* which you can pick up at the S Zaccaria or S Marco landing stage. *Vaporetto* literally means little steamer though these days they run on diesel. Despite its name – the *accelerato*, No 1 is the slow boat down the

canal, stopping at every landing stage. Buy a ticket at the landing stage and take a boat heading in the Piazzale Roma direction. Make sure you sit on the left-hand side, ideally in one of the coveted seats in the prow.

The *Canalazzo*, as Venetians call the Grand Canal, provides a parade of well over 100 *palazzo* façades, from the finely restored to the sadly dilapidated. Roughly 2 miles (3.2km) long, it sweeps through the heart of the city and teems with traffic of all descriptions, from gondolas to garbage barges. Guarding the entrance of the Grand Canal, just beyond the Customs House on the left-hand side, is the all-pervading church of **S Maria della Salute**, Longhena's baroque masterpiece with its huge, exuberant façade, its scrolls and statues and its massive dome. When the boat stops at S Maria del Giglio (right bank), look across to the delightful **Palazzo Dario** with inlaid coloured marble and crowned by distinctive chimney pots. Two buildings further on is the **Palazzo Venier dei Leoni**, an incongruous two-storeyed white structure known as the Palazzo Nonfinito (unfinished palace). Owners of the **Ca' Grande** on the opposite bank, whose view over the lagoon it would have blocked, put a stop to further building. Nonfinito now houses the **Guggenheim Collection of Modern Art** (see *Pick & Mix* Itinerary 4).

The first bridge you pass under is the wooden **Ponte dell'Accademia**, built as a temporary structure in the 1930s but retained by popular demand. Behind the Accademia stop stands the **Scuola della Carità**, housing the Accademia gallery with the world's finest collection of Venetian paintings (see *Pick & Mix* Itinerary 3). Just beyond the next stop, unmistakable for its monumental stone façade, is Longhena's **Ca' Rezzonico**, arguably the finest Baroque palace in Venice (see *Pick & Mix* Itinerary 4). Almost opposite this,

Grand Canal vista

on the right bank, is the white stone **Palazzo Grassi**, an excellent example of an 18th-century nobleman's residence, now owned by Fiat and used for occasional art exhibitions.

On the canal bend, just before the main tributary to the left (the Rio Foscari), stands the **Ca' Foscari**, described by Ruskin as 'the noblest example in Venice of 15th-century Gothic'. On the far side of the *rio* stands the **Palazzo Balbi**, an imposing late 16th-century palace (distinguished by a pair of pinnacles) enjoying one of the most scenic spots on the canal. Napoleon watched a regatta here in his honour in 1807. As you stop at the S Tomà landing stage, look across to the right to the **Palazzo Mocinego**. Byron rented the place for £200 a year, his affair with his housekeeper ('of considerable beauty and energy . . . but wild as a witch and fierce as a demon') ended with the brandishing of knives and the lady flinging herself into the Grand Canal. Directly after the S Angelo landing stage, look right to the **Palazzo Corner Spinelli**, a Renaissance gem designed by Mauro Coducci, distinguished by its round-headed windows and rusticated ground floor. Some consider it the finest Renaissance *palazzo* in Venice. Shortly before the S Silvestro landing stage, the large and austere building on the right is the **Palazzo Grimari**, a Renaissance masterpiece by Michele Sanmichele, which now houses the Courts of Appeal.

Enjoy the ride until the Rialto landing stage, where you disembark. Walk up the bridge to watch the activity below: gondolas, launches, *vaporetti*, barges, garbage collectors and small skiffs. The first structure to span the Grand Canal was a wooden drawbridge which was built in the 12th century but collapsed under the weight of crowds. When a second drawbridge gave way, plans were made for a stone bridge. Competition for the design was fierce, with Michelangelo, Palladio and Sansovino contending. However it was the appropriately named Antonio da Ponte who won. The bridge was built 28m (92ft) high, to allow for the great galleys. Until 1854 this was the only way of crossing the Grand Canal on foot.

Stroll around or choose a canalside café for a drink, then make your way back to Piazza San Marco via the **Mercerie**. Return to the Campo San Salvatore and follow the yellow signs for San Marco. If

Rialto market

they lead you in two directions, not to worry. All roads eventually lead to the Piazza San Marco. The **Mercerie** has been a main shopping thoroughfare for centuries and the streets were lined with fabulous oriental fabrics.

Arriving back in Piazza San Marco in the late afternoon or early evening it is tempting to sit down at an elegant café terrace to watch the evening *passeggiata*. Try **Quadri's** opposite, the favourite of Austrian officers during the occupation – and as a result still shunned by some Venetians. They probably chose this one because it was – and still is – sunny all day.

Alternatively, if you are feeling affluent, treat yourself to a *Bellini* (champagne and peach juice) at **Harry's Bar** right behind the San Marco landing stage. Cuisine here is still regarded as among the best in Venice but it is fiendishly expensive, so when it comes to dinner why not move away from San Marco and try the **Al Covo** (Campiello della Pescaria Castello 3968; Tel: 522 3812; closed Wednesday and Thursday). This is on a tiny square off the Riva degli Schiavoni, the other side of the piazza. It is one of the few places where all the fish is fresh from the lagoon. No language problems here – the enthusiastic Diane Benelli, who runs the place with her Italian husband, comes from the United States.

Night-time view of the Campanile from Quadri's café

Piazza, Paintings and Palaces

This triangular tour takes you from Piazza San Marco to two other focal points of Venice: the Accademia Gallery, housing the world's finest collection of Venetian art, and the Dorsoduro, one of the most charming neighbourhoods in the city.

Begin your day at Piazza San Marco to absorb a little more of this sumptuous square. The eye will inevitably be drawn to the Basilica and you may like to spend another half hour or so picking out details you missed on Day 1. Spare some time for the **Piazzetta**, the sunny square with splendid views across to the island of San Giorgio Maggiore. Admire the architectural masterpieces of Sansovino, who was the city's leading architect until the arrival of Palladio. The **Sansoviniana Library**, praised by Palladio as the richest building since antiquity, is generally acclaimed as his masterpiece. Also by Sansovina is the severe looking **Zecca** or Mint (beside the library and facing the lagoon); and – more in harmony with the libary – the **Loggetta** at the foot of the Campanile.

The two huge columns in the Piazzetta, which were brought from the Orient in the 12th century, are surmounted by statues of the recently restored winged lion of S Marco and S Teodoro, who

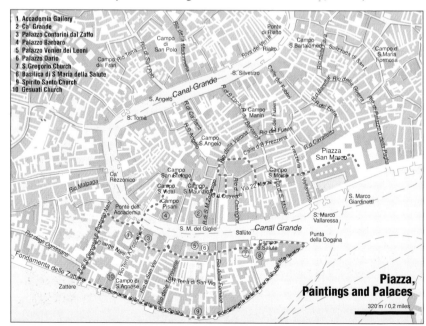

1. Accademia Gallery
2. Ca' Grande
3. Palazzo Contarini dal Zaffo
4. Palazzo Barbaro
5. Palazzo Venier dei Leoni
6. Palazzo Dario
7. S.Gregorio Church
8. Basilica di S Maria della Salute
9. Spirito Santo Church
10. Gesuati Church

**Piazza,
Paintings and Palaces**

320 m / 0,2 miles

The Loggetta at the foot of the Campanile

was the patron saint of Venice until the body of St Mark was brought from Alexandria. The engineer who miraculously managed to set up the columns in 1172 was rewarded with the gambling monopoly in Venice. Executions frequently took place between the pillars and superstitious Venetians never walk between the two.

Leave Piazza San Marco at the western end. For a free map and list of opening times and events call in at the **tourist office** under the arch. The street straight ahead (where shops with big designer names may well divert the eye) will lead you into the Campo S Moisè. Contrast here the overwhelming baroque detail on the church façade and the stark façade of the Bauer Grünwald hotel, one of very few – but very conspicuous – modern intrusions into Venice. Cross the bridge into the Calle Larga 22 Marzo, a wide shopping street named after the day when the patriots reclaimed the Republic from the Austrians during the 1848 uprising.

Teatro La Fenice

Divert north, along the Calle della Veste (or Calle dell Sartor da Veste), over the bridge and into the charming **Campo San Fantin**. To your right stands the late Renaissance church of S Fantin, to the left the **Teatro La Fenice**, whose solemn neoclassical façade hides one of the loveliest opera auditoriums in the world. In 1838 it was almost completely destroyed by fire, but it rose again 'like a phoenix' (*fenice*), rebuilt almost exactly as it used to be. The only way you will see inside the lavish interior is to attend a performance. So, if what is advertised on the posters appeals to you, buy tickets now from the box office. A concert or opera here is an experience you are unlikely to forget. To the left of the Fenice, the house with the open-air staircase was a notorious brothel in the 16th century. Bordering the north of the square the **Ateneo Veneto** was once the headquarters of the Scuola di San Girolamo, a charitable institution, whose members chaperoned criminals to the scaffold and made sure that they were given a proper and decent burial.

Take the street on the far side of the Fenice, where you may hear musicians rehearsing, turn left at the end under the colonnade and cross the bridge. Turn left into the little Campiello dei Calegheri, over the bridge and along the pretty Fondamenta della Fenice where you see the water entrance to the opera house with its blue and yellow mooring posts. The first right turning brings you into the Campo Santa Maria del Giglio, whose church, with its profusion of baroque ornament and secular statuary, appalled Ruskin. Stop here to see the painting by Rubens inside the chapel.

Turn right out of the square and follow the yellow signs for the Accademia until you come to the large, rambling **Campo San Stefano**, otherwise known as the Campo Francesco Morosini. This was the site of the last bullfight in 1802. Stop here for coffee, preferably at **Paulin**, almost opposite the church. Their ice creams are excellent. In the centre of the square is a 19th-century statue of Nicolò Tommaseo, the courageous Dalmatian scholar who, along with

The view from Campo San Vio

Palazzo Barbaro

Daniele Manin, led Venetian resistance against her Austrian rulers.

As you come south from the square cast a glance left at the massive **Palazzo Pisani**, a rarity in that its *campo* façade is as fine as that facing the canal. Pass the deconsecrated church of S Vidal on your right, then note the red house on the far side of the *rio* where Aldous Huxley wrote part of *Brave New World*. Stop on the Accademia bridge for splendid views of the Salute. On the far side of the bridge turn right for the **Accademia** gallery, the world's richest collection of Venetian painting. Spend between one and two hours here using *Pick & Mix* Itinerary 3 as your guide.

Lunch involves a brief but worthwhile detour to the **Antica Locanda Montin** (closed Wednsday), a charming trattoria west of the gallery. Turn left as you come out following the yellow signs for Piazzale Roma and Ferrovia. Follow the general flow across the Ponte delle Maravegie, carry straight on past bars, shops and the Libreria alla Toletta, a good bookshop. At the small bridge, by a *pasticceria*, turn left. At the canal another left turn will bring you down to the restaurant. The walls of this ex-haunt of writers and artists are covered with paintings, some exchanged for free meals. Sit here or in the garden under the vine for *antipasto Montin*, *malfatti alla panna* (delicious creamy pasta), grilled fish fresh from the Adriatic and *tiramisù*, an alcoholic chocolate and coffee gâteau.

The afternoon is for leisurely strolling, browsing in boutiques and bookshops or exploring secluded corners that lie off the main thoroughfares. Begin with the eastern section of the Dorsoduro, a smart residential quarter of pretty sunlit squares, narrow canals and hidden gardens. Start at the Accademia and work eastwards, zigzagging behind Grand Canal *palazzi*. Pause at **Campo San Vio**, sit on the red bench beside the Grand Canal (seats in the city are a rare bonus) and watch the activity on the water. Look across to the right at the massive **Ca' Grande**, whose owners, the Corner family,

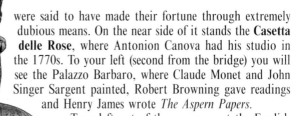

were said to have made their fortune through extremely dubious means. On the near side of it stands the **Casetta delle Rose**, where Antonion Canova had his studio in the 1770s. To your left (second from the bridge) you will see the Palazzo Barbaro, where Claude Monet and John Singer Sargent painted, Robert Browning gave readings and Henry James wrote *The Aspern Papers*.

Turn left out of the square, past the English Church, whose doors were made out of British World War I cannons, and follow the street till you come to the back of the Palazzo Venier dei Leoni, housing the **Guggenheim Collection of Modern Art**. You can spend an hour here (see *Pick & Mix* Itinerary 4) or come back on a Saturday evening, from 6pm–9pm when entrance is free. Carry on to **Campiello Barbaro**, a pretty square with three acacia trees, a print shop, a frame shop, and views of the chimney pots on the Palazzo Dario. Pass the Salviati glass showrooms in a grand palace setting and, further along, more glass at Cenedese where you can watch glass-blowing. In the Campo San Gregorio the deconsecrated Gothic brick church of San Gregorio is now used as a workshop for restoring paintings. Its former

Basilica da Santa Maria della Salute

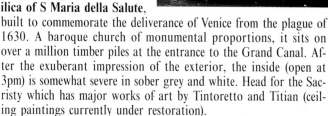

monastery lies to the left. The doorway of No 172 hides what Ruskin described as 'the loveliest *cortile* I know in Venice'.

Cross over a tiny bridge to Longhena's great domed **Basilica of S Maria della Salute**, built to commemorate the deliverance of Venice from the plague of 1630. A baroque church of monumental proportions, it sits on over a million timber piles at the entrance to the Grand Canal. After the exuberant impression of the exterior, the inside (open at 3pm) is somewhat severe in sober grey and white. Head for the Sacristy which has major works of art by Tintoretto and Titian (ceiling paintings currently under restoration).

If you follow the embankment beyond the Salute you will find yourself at the **Punta della Dogana**, where a golden globe supports the charming figure of Fortuna, forming a weathervane. The ability to combine elegance and practicality (as in the gondola) is typical of Venetian genius. From the tip of the Dorsoduro you can take in the great sights of San Marco, the island of San Giorgio Maggiore and the landmarks along Giudecca. The multinational Guggenheim conglomerate have their eye on the disused customs houses behind you – a prime site for another gallery.

Follow the waterside to the **Zattere**, the long stone-flagged quayside skirting the Giudecca Canal. *Zattere* means rafts and orig-

inates from the days when timber was moored here. It is an open, sunny spot to look across to the island of Giudecca or watch the activity of boats in the choppy Giudecca Canal. Pass the Calcina Pensione where Ruskin stayed as an old man. If the **Gesuati church** is open, stop to see the ceiling frescoed by Tiepolo, an early work already showing his mastery of light and perspective.

Choose a café terrace and watch the waterbuses chugging across to Giudecca. If it is sunny, while away the early evening and eat at one of the waterside restaurants – either a bowl of pasta at one of the simpler establishments or something more elaborate at the **Riviera Restaurant** at No 1473. The chef here trained at Harry's Bar but you only pay a fraction of the cost of the more flash establishment. Try any of the home made pastas – *gnocchi al gorgonzola* is excellent, so is steamed salmon with fried *zucchini*, washed down with a bottle of Prosecco.

DAY 3

Quiet Corners of Castello

A day exploring the eastern region of Venice, known as Castello. Start at the bustling waterfront close to San Marco, work your way north to the great Gothic church of Santi Giovanni e Paolo, passing through quiet streets and squares. The tour covers some of the finest art and architectural treasures in the city and ends with a choice of 'cicheti' (snacks) in a Venetian wine bar or a slap-up meal in one of the best restaurants in the city.

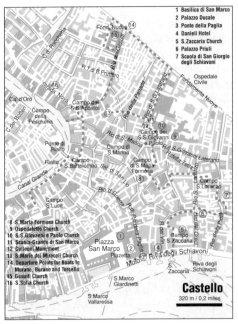

1 Basilica di San Marco
2 Palazzo Ducale
3 Ponte della Paglia
4 Danieli Hotel
5 S.Zaccaria Church
6 Palazzo Priuli
7 Scuola di San Giorgio degli Schiavoni

8 S.Maria Formosa Church
9 Ospedaletto Church
10 S.S.Giovanni e Paolo Church
11 Scuola-Grande di San Marco
12 Colleoni Monument
13 S.Maria dei Miracoli Church
14 Departure Points for Boats to Murano, Burano and Torcello
15 Gesuiti Church
16 S.Sofia Church

Castello
320 m / 0,2 miles

Start the morning at the **Molo**, the busy waterfront south of Palazzo Ducale, where gondolas sway by the quayside and camera-clicking crowds admire the views across the water to the shimmering island of San Giorgio Maggiore. Pick your way through stalls of souvenirs and easels of lightning sketch-artists and cross the Ponte della Paglia. Look left for the **Bridge of Sighs**. Cross the bridge to the **Riva degli Schiavoni**, a curving promenade skirting the *sestiere* of Castello, named after the Dalmatian sailors who used to moor their trading boats and barges along the waterfront. It is still a scene of intense activity, as *vaporetti, motoscafi*, barges, tugs and cruisers moor at the landing stages and ferries chug across to the islands. On a sunny day this is a lovely spot to stop for morning coffee, preferably at an open-air terrace with uninterrupted views across the lagoon (but beware the prices!).

Beyond the former prisons, the luxury **Danieli Hotel** occupies the Gothic Palazzo Dandolo and the modern aberration next door. The hotel has occupied the main building since 1822 and in that time has opened its door to many an illustrious visitor, including Wagner, Ruskin, Balzac, Proust and Dickens, who took delight in describing, the horrors of the prisons next door.

Wedding in the church of San Zaccharia

Cross over the colonnaded Ponte del Vin and take the second turning to the left, under the *sotoportego* signposted to San Zaccaria. This brings you to a quiet *campo*, flanked on one side by the part-Gothic and part-Renaissance façade of the church of **San Zaccaria**. The upper section, by leading Renaissance architect, Mauro Coducci, is particularly fine. In the 16th century the adjoining convent – not unlike other convents in the city – was notorious for its riotous, amoral nuns.

Inside the church, start with the chapels and crypt, reached by an entrance on the right-hand side of the church. If closed apply to the custodian. The Chapel of St Athanasius, with paintings by Titian, Tintoretto and Palma Vecchio, leads to the **Chapel of S Tarasio**, the former chancel, whose vault is decorated with frescoes by the Florentine master, Andrea Castagno. The crypt, sometimes flooded, lies below. The greatest work of art is in the main church: Giovanni Bellini's glorious *Sacre Conversazione* above the first altarpiece on the left in the main church. This is one of the very finest paintings in Venice – a compelling work where the serene, meditative figures are integrated by soft shadow and rich, mellow hues.

Leave the church and the square via the archway. Turn right into Campo San Provolo, go under the *sottoportico* and, just beyond a beadshop, you will come into the Fondamenta dell'Osmarin (*osmarin* meaning rosemary). On a corner on the far side of the canal

Riva degli Schiavoni

Campo di Santa Maria Formosa

is the redbrick **Palazzo Priuli**, one of the finest Venetian Gothic palaces. At the end of the canal cross the two bridges and look right to the church of **S Giorgio dei Greci** with its tall, distinctly tilted belltower. Take the narrow alley straight ahead, pass the pretty Campiello de la Fraterna on the left and join the Salizza da dei Greci. The **Trattoria Da Remigio** this end is excellent value. At the far end of the street cross over the bridge and immediately turn left. Follow the canal along the Fondamenta dei Furlani and you will come face to face with the **Scuola di San Giorgio degli Schiavoni** (closed Monday), founded by the Dalmatians to protect their community in Venice. The *scuola* is tiny, but it is decorated by an an exquisite frieze of paintings by Carpaccio illustrating the lives of the Dalmatian patron saints, St George, St Tryphon and St Jerome. The scenes are rich in colour, remarkably vivid and detailed and give you a good idea of what life was like in Venice and the Veneto at the turn of the 16th century.

Coming out of the Scuola, cross the bridge and turn right following the canal northwards. Just before a portico take a left turn down the Calle San Lorenzo for the church of **San Lorenzo**, which is now a hospice. Marco Polo is said to have been buried here but his tomb was lost when the church was rebuilt in 1592. Cross the bridge at the other side of the square, turn immediately right, then first left down the Borgoloco San Lorenzo. Cross the canal of San Severo, pausing on the bridge to see some fine *pallazi* on the far side, pass under the dark and

Campo Santi Giovanni e Paolo

narrow *sotto portego*, carry straight on, then take a right turn for the lovely **Campo di Santa Maria Formosa**.

This large rambling square, once the site of bullfights and open-air theatre, is full of Venetian life, with children playing and daily market stalls selling fruit and vegetables. It is flanked by beautiful *palazzi* and dominated by the swelling apses of Coducci's church of **Santa Maria Formosa**. *Formosa*, meaning both beautiful and buxom, seems appropriate.

If you are ready for lunch, pizzerias in the square provide a cheerful, open-air setting. For something more authentic try the **Al Mascaron** at No 5223, Calle Lunga Santa Maria Formosa, the narrow street to the east of the square. It is an inconspicuous old-fashioned *osteria* where you will find well-prepared snacks, excellent fish, good wines and lots of locals. Solid wooden tables and paper tablecloths are the order of the day. Save coffee until you come to the **Campo Santi Giovanni e Paolo** to the north. Take the tiny street almost opposite Al Mascaron, cross a quiet canal and go straight on until you come to the square. Sit at one of the cafés this side to absorb the wealth of architecture and sculpture around you and imagine the splendour of the scene in the days when the square bordered the waters of the lagoon.

On your right is the church of **SS Giovanni e Paolo**, more familiarly known as San Zanipolo. This huge brick edifice vies with the Frari as the greatest Gothic church in Venice. After the tiny streets of Castello its towering, austere form makes a dramatic impact. Next to it and facing you is the beautiful rich Renaissance façade of the **Scuola Grande di San Marco**, once the meeting house

Scuola Grande di San Marco

of silk dealers and goldsmiths, now the civic hospital (ambulances are usually moored in the adjoining canal). Look at the *trompe l'oeil* arches framing lions that appear to be looking from the far end of deep Renaissance porticos – in fact they are barely 6 inches (152mm) deep. Closer to, on a pedestal, stands what is considered one of the finest Renaissance sculptures: **the equestrian statue of Bartolomeo Colleoni**, by Verrocchio. A famous *condottiere*, Colleoni was immensely rich and offered the city of Venice a huge sum of money if they granted him an equestrian monument 'in front of San Marco'. This ran contrary to Venetian tradition but, eager to get their hands on Colleoni's fortune, the government found the answer: since the will did not stipulate the Basilica, the statue would stand in front of the Scuola San Marco instead.

The church doors open at 3.30pm. The interior of this stately Gothic structure is remarkably spacious. Known as the Pantheon of Venice, it contains the tombs of 25 doges. Identifying them is impossible without a detailed guide or the official booklet, which you can buy in the sacristy. Finest of all is Tullio Lombardo's *Monument to Doge Andrea Vendramin* (1476–8) on the left hand side of the apse. The figures are exquisitely graceful and beautiful, yet at the same time natural and unaffected. To the left compare the Gothic *Monument to Doge Marco Corner*, by Nino Pisano, executed 110 years earlier. Paintings to single out are Giovanni Bellini's *St Vincent Ferrer* polyptych over the second altar on the right; G B Piazzetta's glowing *Apotheosis of San Dominico* on the ceiling of the San Domenico chapel (third chapel on the right); and the Veronese ceiling paintings in the Rosary Chapel.

Cross the bridge opposite the church for a brief detour to the exquisite church of **Santa Maria dei Miracoli**. Go over the next bridge and walk on to the Ponte del Povan, a lovely spot with views of three canals. Just beyond you will see the delightful geometric marble façade of the Miracoli. One glimpse and you will begin to understand why all Venetians want to get married here.

Return to the Campo dei SS Giovanni e Paolo and fol-

Doge's Mausoleum, San Zanipolo

Ceiling of Santa Maria dei Miracoli

low the Fondamenta dei Mendicanti (Beggars' Embankment) northwards, along the side of the hospital. You soon come to the **Fondamente Nuove** with splendid views of the lagoon and a refreshing breeze. Turn left, cross the bridge and look across to the island of San Michele where the walls of the cemetery are set against a backdrop of dark leaning cypresses. Stravinsky, Ezra Pound and Diaghilev are all buried there. These are among the lucky ones that retain their graves. Most corpses are dug up after 10–12 years and taken to a public ossuary.

Cross the bridge beyond the last landing stage and leave the quayside by turning left (signposted San Marco). This takes you past the baroque façade of the **Gesuiti church**, with statues of the Twelve Apostles. It has an elaborate green and white marble interior containing Titian's famous *Martyrdom of St Lawrence*. At this point you should follow the yellow signs for the Rialto. As you approach the bridge, spare time for at least a cursory glance at the church of **S Giovanni Cristostomo**, crammed into a little square north of the Rialto. It was Mauro Coducci's last work, built at the turn of the 15th century. Inside there are two outstanding works of art: Giovanni Bellini's *St Jerome with St Christopher and St Augustine*, over the first altar, and Sebastiano del Piombo's painting of *St John Chrysostom and Six Saints* on the high altar.

Enough sights for the day. Spend the early evening strolling down the Rialto and along the Riva del Carbon watching the rush hour on the Grand Canal and soaking up the atmosphere. At the end of this embankment, turn left into Calle Cavalli and look for **Al Volto** (No 4081). This wine-tasting bar is informal, small and very popular, so expect crowds to be spilling out into the street.

Canal by Santa Maria dei Miracoli

Take your pick from 1,300 wines or take pot luck and opt for an *ombra*, a small glass of local wine. Snacks at the Al Volto could fill you up for the evening, but for a more substantial meal try the **Alla Madonna**, Calle della Madonna (the other side of the Rialto), excellent for fresh fish and crab, but be prepared for crowds and brusque service. Or splash out and dine at the **Poste Vecie** (closed Tuesday off season), a charming old trattoria reached by a quaint alley behind the fish market. Pastas are homemade (try the black noodles or *bilgoli in salsa*, with anchovies and onion sauce) and fish is fresh from the market.

Morning Itineraries

1. Markets, Masks and Art

Begin on the spot where the city first started: the Rialto. Browse among market stalls, then wind your way through the tiny alleys of San Polo to the great Gothic church of the Frari. Explore the quarter to the south and see Venetian life in some of the humbler, more remote corners of the city. End the day on the Zattere quayside, looking across the lagoon to the island of Giudecca.

For centuries the Rialto – which to tourists is the bridge and to Venetians is the quarter around it – has been the commercial hub of the city. It was here that the first inhabitants of the lagoon are said to have settled. By the heyday of the republic it was one of the major financial quarters of Europe – a centre for bankers, brokers and merchants who traded in spices and silks.

Rialto market

Make an early start to see the **markets** in full swing and the barges offloading at the quayside by the Grand Canal. Best days to go are Tuesday to Saturday when both markets are functioning.

Start in the Ruga degli Orefici (sign-posted *Oresi*), just north of the bridge, where the stalls create one of the most colourful scenes in Venice: gleaming peppers and aubergines, thick sticks of asparagus, fat red tomatoes, yellow-flowered *zucchini*, bags of lemons and bunches of coriander. With the approach of summer come wild strawberries, plump peaches, cherries, figs

MIX

and water melons – all of which make you wonder why Venetian restaurant menus are so frequently uninspired.

Follow through into the Ruga degli Speziali, the street of the spice traders, where you may catch a whiff of fresh coffee beans and the few spices that are still sold from a couple of grocery stores. At the end of the street turn right for the **Pescheria,** or fish market, where gleaming sardines, sole and skate, sea bass and spider crabs, squid and live shrimps are all laid out in trays under the colonnades. Make for the far side of the market for good views of the Grand Canal and the *palazzi* on the far bank, including the Gothic gem of the Ca' d'Oro.

Walk alongside the fruit and vegetable market on your right, watch the produce being offloaded at the water's edge and carted off to stalls, shops and restaurants. High water permitting, wander along the quayside almost as far as the Rialto Bridge. Then rejoin the Ruga degli Orefici, passing the delightful **S Giacomo di Rialto,** the oldest church in Venice. Retrace your steps along to the Campo

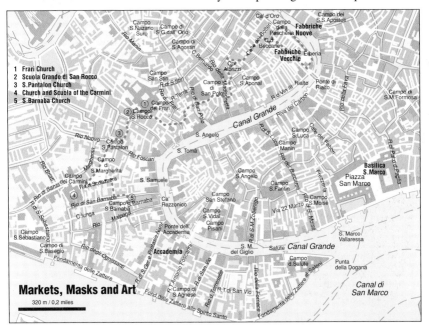

1 Frari Church
2 Scuola Grande di San Rocco
3 S.Pantalon Church
4 Church and Scuola of the Carmini
5 S.Barnaba Church

Markets, Masks and Art

320 m / 0,2 miles

Campo di San Polo, second largest square in Venice

Beccarie and, if the mood takes you, stop for coffee at the **Osteria da Pinto** where fishmongers may be having a morning tipple.

Follow the yellow signs for Piazzale Roma, which will take you over a bridge and into the Calle dei Botteri. Turn left here, ignore any yellow signs and follow the street until it narrows, at which point turn right into the charming little square marked Carampane. Pass under the *sotoportego*, then make a brief diversion by turning right into what is marked as the Rio Terà de la Carampane. The first bridge on your right is the **Ponte delle Tette** or Bridge of the Teats which, they say, is named after the prostitutes – of which there were over 11,000 in Venice in the 16th-century – who used to frequent this quarter, stripping down to the waist to lure their customers into the brothels.

Return to the street you came off and take the first right for the Campiello Albrizzi, a small square flanked on the far side by the well-preserved 18th-century Palazzo Albrizzi. Cross the square and turn left into what must be the narrowest alley in the city. Turn right under the colonnades and over the bridge into the Calle de la Furatola and you will soon reach the main Rialto/Piazzale Roma throughfare. Turn right into the Calle de la Madonnetta, cross the bridge and carry on until you come into the **Campo di San Polo**, the largest square in Venice after Piazza San Marco. It has none of the grandeur of San Marco but is nonetheless beautiful in its own way and hums with Venetian life. Once the site of bullfights, tournaments, masked balls, fairs and festivals, it is now the scene of less exotic activities such as football, rollerskating and cycling.

Next to the church the classical Palazzo Corner Mocenigo was for a while the residence of Frederick Rolfe (self-styled Baron Corvo), the notoriously eccentric English writer. It was here that he wrote *The Desire and Pursuit of the Whole*, ruthlessly lampooning English society in Venice. As a result his host threw him out, pen-

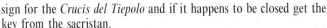

Masks at Tragicomica

niless, on to the streets. On the opposite side of the square is the more striking Palazzo Soranzo with its sweeping pink Gothic façade. The most interesting feature of the church of **San Polo** is a chapel with Giandomenico Tiepolo's evocative paintings of the Stations of the Cross. Follow the sign for the *Crucis del Tiepolo* and if it happens to be closed get the key from the sacristan.

Turn right out of the church, cross the bridge into the Calle dei Saoneri. If the **Trattoria da Ignazio** (No 2749; closed Saturday) appeals, book a table for lunch later on. The fish is excellent and there's a garden at the back. Small shops specialising in leather, lace, prints, masks and other Venetian crafts may tempt you along this and the next two streets. At the end of Calle dei Saoneri, turn left, past a print shop and then right into the Calle dei Nomboli. Half way along the stunning masks at **Tragicomica** invariably catch the attention of passers-by. Every one of them is handmade by craftsmen – hence the prices. Masks range from *Commedia dell'Arte* characters (Harlequin, Punch, etc) to allegorical masks of the creator's own invention. Almost opposite the shop is **Carlo Goldoni's house**. If it is open you can see (free of charge) theatre memorabilia, costumes and relics of this great Venetian playwright. If not, peek into the lovely courtyard through the iron gates.

Take the bridge at the end of the street, cross a small square and you will come into the Campo San Tomà. From here follow the signs for the Scuola Grande di San Rocco. This will bring you into the Campo dei Frari, dominated by the huge brick walls and soaring campanile of the **Frari church**. Along with the church of SS Giovanni e Paolo in Castello, this is the finest Gothic church in Venice. It was built in the 14th and 15th centuries by Franciscan friars whose first principle was poverty – hence the austerity and meagre decoration of the façade. Inside, the church is as good as an art gallery, with an impressive collection. Bear in mind that it closes at noon. You will need coins for the lighting and the recorded commentaries which are better than most. Keep the ticket which has a useful map of the art treasures in the church.

Once inside, the eye is inevitably drawn to Titian's glori-

Titian's 'Assumption of the Virgin'

ously rich *Assumption of the Virgin*, which crowns the main altar. On the entrance side of the church the same artist's *Madonna di Ca' Pèsaro*, is another masterpiece of light, colour and harmony, and a very daring work in that it was one of the very earliest to depict the Madonna out of the centre of the composition. Members of the Pèsaro family, who commissioned the work, can be seen in the lower half of the painting. Directly opposite is Titian's mausoleum, erected 300 years after his death. Other outstanding works of art are Giovanni Bellini's beautiful *Madonna and Child with Saints* in the sacristy, of which Henry James said 'nothing in Venice is more perfect than this'; the finely carved 15th-century monks' choir; the wooden statue by Donatello of St John the Baptist on the altarpiece to the right of the main altar; and, in an entirely different vein, the monument to Canova (to the left of the side door), the design of which was originally created by Canova himself as a monument to Titian.

Turn right out of the church and follow the sign for the neighbouring **Scuola Grande di San Rocco**. This fine Renaissance building contains an unrivalled collection of paintings by Tintoretto. He was one of several eminent contenders for the decoration of the Scuola, among them Veronese; but Tintoretto caught his competitors unaware by producing not merely a plan but a completed painting, already in place on the ceiling of the Conference Room. He worked on the Scuola on and off for 24 years.

Pay your admission charge, collect a free plan of the paintings

Detail from Tintoretto's 'Last Supper', Scuola Grande di San Rocco

and remember the Scuola closes at 1pm. Be warned that the lighting is very poor. As you go round note the artist's extraordinary ability to convey theatrical effect through contrasts of light and shade, bold foreshortening, visionary effects of colour and unusual viewpoints. In the lower hall the paintings illustrate scenes from the *Life of the Virgin*, while the upper hall has paintings over 4.8m (16ft) high depicting scenes from the *Life of Christ* and, on the ceiling, scenes from the Old Testament. In the Sala dell'Albergo, at the far end, scenes from the Passion culminate in *The Crucifixion* itself, fittingly the largest, most moving and intensely dramatic painting of the collection. The *Glorification of St Roch* on the ceiling of the same room was the work which won Tintoretto the commission.

For lunch return to **Ignazio** (see above) or try **Da Fiore** north of the Campo San Polo (closed Sunday, Monday and August) in Calle del Scaleter 2202, an elegant little restaurant, off the beaten track and excellent for fish. If, after lunch, you feel like exploring the western part of the Dorsoduro return to the Campo San Rocco, take the Calle Fianco della Scuola beside the Scuola, then cross the bridge and walk to the end of the Calle della Scuola. Turn left and immediately right into Calle San Pantalon which brings you into the square of the same name. The church has a huge ceiling fresco by Fumiani. On the left-hand side of the square, close to the canal, spot the old slab which lists varieties of fish and the minimum sizes they had to reach before they were allowed to be sold. Cross the bridge over the Rio Foscari and walk down to the **Campo di Santa Margherita**, a fine rectangular 'square' bustling with local life. **Causin** at the near end has particularly good ice creams.

The square tapers at the far end and brings you to the **church and Scuola of the Carmini**. The Scuola houses Tiepolo's sensational ceiling painting, *St Simon Stock Receiving the Scapular of the Carmelite Order from the Virgin*. The Carmelites were so pleased with it that they made Tiepolo an honorary member of the Scuola.

Floating market

Coming back into the square keep to the right and follow the yellow signs for Accademia which take you into the Rio Terrà Canal. Look out on the right for the mask shop **Mondonovo** with an extraordinary range of fantasy faces. As you approach the canal of San Barnaba you will see, on the far side, one of the last surviving floating vegetable markets. Cross the bridge into **Campo San Barnaba**, traditionally a quarter for the impoverished nobility. Look out for craftsmen binding books, restoring antiques and creating carnival masks.

Sit back and enjoy a ride on the ferry-steamer No 5. This circular tour around the periphery of Venice provides some stunning scenery and will renew the spirits after an overdose of sightseeing in the city. In northern Venice discover the oldest ghetto in the world and the lovely quarter of Madonna dell'Orto; complete the circle by returning via the Arsenale.

Catch a No 5 *vaporetto* from the S Zaccaria landing stage, east of Piazza San Marco and make sure it is marked *circolare destra*. You can either purchase a ticket for a single journey and do the same for each leg of the trip, or invest in a Day Pass which entitles you to unlimited travel for 24 hours on all lines except No 2.

The boat veers out into the San Marco Canal towards the **island of San Giorgio Maggiore**. If you have not already seen the church and the views from its campanile, now is the time to do so. The boat will conveniently drop you right by the steps leading up to the church. The boat makes three stops on the **island of Giudecca**. This narrow, gently curving strip of land, made up of eight islands, serves as a suburb to Venice. Opinions differ as to the origins of the name, but the most likely theory is that it stems from the word *giudicati* (meaning judged), dating back to the days when troublesome aristocrats were banished here.

The effect of San Giorgio Maggiore

The island has a working fishing community, splendid views across to Venice and three churches of merit. The *vaporetto* stops at *Zitelle*, named after the nearby church of the same name, also designed by Palladio. But the architect's most splendid church is the **Redentore** which you can see if you alight at the next stop. The great dome is one of the most conspicuous landmarks of Venice and the interior, strikingly stark and solemn, is a supreme example of classical rationality. The church was built to to commemorate the deliverance of Venice from the plague in 1576 which took 50,000 lives.

After the S Eufemia stop, the boat angles right across the canal to the **Zattere**. On a sunny day the quayside will lure you with its open-air cafés and views across to Giudecca. Stretch your legs along the quayside, see the Tiepolo ceiling in the Gesuati church,

The Redentore's dome is one of Venice's landmarks

then return to the landing stage to take another No 5 *vaporetto* (*circolare destra*). After S Basilio, the boat will recross the Giudecca Canal and stop at the unexciting island of Sacca Fisola. As you approach you can't fail to notice the massive neo-Gothic **Mulino Stucky**, formerly a flour mill, now a ruin. From here the boat rounds the western end of Venice through docklands, then suddenly hits the Grand Canal. After the railway station stop you pass under the bridge of the Scalzi, then turn left up the Canale di Cannaregio, the main entrance into Venice before the advent of the Ponte della Libertà. Look left for the **Palazzo Labia**, once home of the extraordinarily rich Labia family, now the headquarters of RAI, the broadcasting network.

Disembark at Guglie, the stop just after the stone and brick bridge. This is a lively area of Cannaregio with waterside stalls, small shops and trattorias. This northern arc of Venice, known as **Cannaregio**, is one of the most fascinating but least explored areas. The word *Cannaregio* comes from *canne*, meaning reeds and dates back to the days when all this territory was marshland. As you get off the boat turn left, go under the archway immediately on your right signposted Sinagoghe, which will take you past fascinating small workshops and local bars to the **Ghetto Vecchio** and the **Campo de la Scuola**. Continue, over a bridge into the **Campo del Ghetto Nuovo**, which, despite the name, is the world's oldest ghetto and the one that gave its name to isolated Jewish communities throughout the world.

In the early 16th century Jews in Venice were confined to one of the islands of Cannaregio and the only answer to their cramped conditions was to build

Palazzo Labia (with square tower)

upwards. Hence the 'skyscrapers' of Venice, tenement blocks of five or six storeys which used to be the highest blocks in Europe. The site was an iron foundry where cannons were made and the word *ghetto* comes from *getare* meaning to cast. The community remained on the site until 1797 when Napoleon had the gates torn down and from then on Jews could live where they liked. Only a few Jewish families still live here.

The most striking feature of the large, rambling **Campo del Ghetto Nuovo** is the series of evocative bas-reliefs by Arbit Blatas, recording the Nazi holocaust. You will see them on the near side of the square, below symbolic strips of barbed wire. On the far side of the square you can visit the **Museo della Comunità Ebraica** (closed Saturday). Guided tours of the synagogues leave at 10.30am, 11.30am and 12.30am.

Take the northern exit from the square and cross the bridge into the Fondamenta degli Ormesini. Turn right along this bustling quayside, past small shops, local bars and trattorias. Turn left down a narrow alley when you see the blue sign 'Ospedale', cross the bridge and turn right along the pretty Fondamenta della Sensa. The cheap prices and picturesque canalside setting of the **Ostaria alla Pergola** may well tempt you to return here for lunch.

Follow the *fondamenta* as far as the **Campo dei Mori.** The statues here are said to depict merchants of the Mastelli family who came to Venice in the 12th century from the Peloponnese. Following the waterside, past another turbaned merchant in a niche in the wall, and you will come to **Tintoretto's house** (No 3399), marked with a plaque and bas-relief of the artist. The painter lived here with his family for many years. Return to the Campo dei Mori,

Tintoretto's house

Classic views of Venice along the Riva degli Schiavoni

cross the bridge on the far side and turn right for views of the charming relief of a one-legged man and a camel which has given this palace its popular name of the Palazzo del Cammello.

Retrace a few steps for the church of **Madonna dell'Orto,** a masterpiece of Venetian Gothic, conspicuous for its oriental campanile, warm brick façade and delightful carved portal. Thanks to the British Venice in Peril Fund it has been (and continues to be) painstakingly restored. The church closes at noon but you may just have time to see the Tintoretto paintings inside. It was the artist's parish church and he is buried in the first chapel on the right.

Wander around this quiet neighbourhood where washing flaps in the breeze and cats doze in sunlit squares. *Orto* means kitchen garden and it is one of the very few areas of Venice where gardens are a feature. Unless you have decided to stay for lunch, make for the Madonna dell'Orto landing stage on the northern embankment. To get there take the street west of the church and zigzag up.

Catch another No 5 *vaporetto* and change boats at the next stop, Fondamente Nuove. Here make sure you pick up Line 5 going in the direction of Giudecca/San Marco (clearly marked on the landing stage). The boat speeds along the Fondamente Nuove, then swings sharp right, with a loud hoot, down into the **Arsenale**. This is the only way to see inside the walls of this once-splendid shipyard. Today it is hard to imagine the great galleys that were once built and fitted out here to protect Venice's maritime commerce. Outside, the boat turns right and sweeps along the Riva degli Schiavoni, affording a splendid panorama of the classic perspectives of Venice, until it drops you at S Zaccaria.

Gentile Bellini's 'Corpus Domini Procession' in the Accademia

3. The Accademia Gallery – A Feast of Venetian Art

'If only the Venetians learnt to draw at a young age…' remarked Michelangelo. They may not have been the greatest draughtsmen but Venetians certainly knew how to paint. See for yourself in the Accademia gallery, the world's richest repository of Venetian art.

The paintings in the gallery are dependent on natural light, so preferably choose a bright morning and be at the gallery as close as you can to 9am. The later you leave it the more crowded it will be, particularly in high season. Note the gallery closes at 2pm on weekdays, 1pm on Sundays. Currently it is open every day but check before you go. The masterpieces, housed in the monastic complex of the S Maria della Carità, are too numerous to absorb in one visit and this itinerary concentrates on just some of the very finest pictures. The most useful guide is *The Galleries of the Accademia* by Francesco Valcanover, available at the book stall in ROOM XXIV, also accessible from ROOM I. Be prepared for paintings or whole rooms closed off for restoration. Room numbering is not always clear. Look on the inside wall if you can't see the room number from the outside.

ROOM I shows the heavy influence of the Byzantine on the earliest Venetian painters. The principal exponent of the style in Venice was **Paolo Veneziana**. One of the most important of his works is the *Coronation of the Virgin* (freestanding, centre), a polyptych with extravagant use of gold. Just before the steps up

'Madonna of the Little Trees', by Giovanni Bellini

to ROOM II, look at the detailed rendering of figures in **Michele Giambono's** *Coronation of the Virgin* – a good example of the International Gothic style.

ROOM II contains one of the most important altarpieces of the early Venetian Renaissance: **Giovanni Bellini's** *Madonna Enthroned with Saints* (right wall). Renaissance painting came late to Venice, brought largely through the great genius **Mantegna**. Giovanni Bellini was his brother-in-law and he, in turn, influenced all the Venetian painters of his own and the following generation. Bellini broke away from the traditional polyptych and brought the Virgin and saints together in a single natural composition. This painting had a vital influence on **Vittore Carpaccio's** *Presentation of Jesus in the Temple* and **Marco Basaiti's** *Christ Praying in the Garden*, both in the same room. All three were painted for the church of S Giobbe.

Skip ROOM III and concentrate on the gems in **ROOM IV** and **ROOM V**. Giovanni Bellini was the greatest of the Venetian Madonna painters. His *Madonna and Child with St Catherine and St Mary Magdalene* (on the right as you go in) demonstrates his masterly balance of naturalness, reality and beauty. In the same room (left wall as you go in) Mantegna's *St George* typifies the dry rationality of the artist's *quattrocento* style. Follow through into ROOM V for further masterpieces

Titian's 'St John the Baptist'

by **Giovanni Bellini**, including the lovely *Madonna of the Little Trees* and *Madonna and Child with John the Baptist and a Saint*. In his evocative *Pietà*, Bellini makes striking use of landscape.

In the same room is one of the very great works of the Venetian Renaissance: *The Tempest* by **Giorgione**. Little is known about the artist and he died of the plague very young, but he is ranked as one of the founders of modern painting. He was an innovator in that he achieved his effect through the use of colour and light as opposed to line and drawing. *The Tempest* is one of the artist's few certain attributions, but the subject still remains a mystery. Beside it, *The Old Woman* by the same artist is a striking piece of early realism.

Turn left for **ROOM VI**. This and the adjoining **ROOMS VII** and **VIII** concentrate on the early 16th century when the Venetian Renaissance was well into its stride. In **ROOM VI**, **Titian** boldly presents *St John the Baptist* as a muscular athlete in a theatrical pose. After the

death of Giorgione (1510), Titian (1487/9–1576) went on to dominate Venetian painting throughout his long life. Brilliant use of colour and lyrical composition are the ingredients of his genius. Typical of the first half of the 16th century are the richly coloured, exuberant paintings such as *The Presentation of the Ring* by **Paris Bordone** (ROOM VI) and the *Sacre Conversazione* by **Palma Vecchio** in (ROOM VIII). On an entirely different note is the melancholy and penetrating *Portrait of a Young Man* by **Lorenzo Lotto** in ROOM VII, left wall. Acute observation of personality is a feature of Venetian Renaissance portraiture.

Take the steps up to ROOM X where three of the greatest Venetian masters are represented. To your right and covering the entire wall is **Veronese's** grandiose *Feast in the House of Levi*. It was painted as *The Last Supper* but its hedonistic content (dogs, drunkards, dwarfs, etc) brought Veronese before the Inquisition. Rather than eliminate the offending details, the painter merely changed the title.

Tintoretto (1518–94) was born in Venice and, unlike Titian, never moved from her shores. A man of fanatical religious conviction, he brought a kind of frenetic mannerism to the Renaissance. His reputation was made with the striking *St Mark Rescuing the Slave* which you see on the opposite wall as you go in. Inspired use of shadow, foreshortening, depth and movement are typified in the dramatic *Stealing of the Body of St Mark* and *St Mark saving a Saracen from Shipwreck*. In the same room, **Titian's** dark sober *Pietà*, bathed in mystic light, was the artist's last work.

ROOM XI displays some sumptuous works by **Veronese.** The *Marriage of St Catherine* and *Madonna Enthroned with Saints* are radiant, richly coloured works demonstrating his use of dazzling hues. At the end of the room you can't miss Tiepolo's grandiose *tondo*, *Discovery of the True Cross*, showing his mastery of illusionistic perspective.

ROOM XII is a gallery of light-hearted, lyrical, almost sugary landscape paintings. During the 18th century the key note in art was to delight and please the senses. Good examples are the graceful, airy *Rape of Europa* and *Apollo and Marsia* by **Tiepolo** (ROOM XVI). As a young man Tiepolo was influenced by **Piazzetta**, whose dashing use of *chiaroscuro* in freehandling style is seen in his masterpiece, *The Soothsayer* (ROOM XVIA).

Topographical painting, as illustrated

in ROOM XVII, was a fashion of the time. Antonio Canal, better known as **Canaletto**, transformed the fashion into an industry. *Perspective* is a good example of his precisely drawn and perspectively accurate scenes. For an intimate insight into Venetian daily life in the 18th century take a look at **Pietro Longhi's** charming, witty, sometimes ironic genre paintings towards the end of the room.

Now you go back in time. Three left turns should bring you to ROOM XX containing eight large canvases by five 'ceremonial artists' of the late 15th/early 16th century, commissioned by the *Scuole Grande di S Giovanni Evangelista*. The scenes, depicting stories of *The True Cross* are not only important as works of art but are full of historical detail, documenting the life, customs and appearance of Venice in the 15th century. Worth singling out are the *Corpus Domini Procession* by **Gentile Bellini** (illustrated on the previous pages) showing Piazza San Marco at the end of the 15th century and the *The Curing of a Man possessed by Demons* by **Carpaccio**, (currently under restoration) showing the old wooden Rialto bridge which collapsed in 1444.

Go back through ROOM XIX and turn left, past the book shop for the last room, ROOM XXIV. On the right the great tryptych of **Antonio Vivarini** and **Giovanni d'Alemagna** demonstrates a combination of the International Gothic and the emerging Renaissance styles. Facing you **Titian's** *The Presentation of the Virgin*, still occupying its original position on the entrance wall of the gallery, makes a fitting finale to your visit.

Have you ever wondered what it was like to live on the Grand Canal? This morning's tour of three palazzi converted to museums will give you some idea.

Your morning starts at the **Ca' d'Oro** (open mornings only) the most magnificent Gothic palace in Venice. From San Marco it is the first stop on a No. 1 *vaporetto* after the Rialto. The lace-like façade with its ogee windows, carved capitals, crowning pinnacles and bas-reliefs was once covered in gold leaf – hence the name, House of Gold.

Palazzo Ca' d'Oro

From the landing stage take the narrow *calle* and you will see the entrance to the gallery on the left. Pause in the picturesque main courtyard with the open stairway and Bartolomeo Bon's beautifully carved red Verona marble well-head. Of the Renaissance masterpieces on the first floor of the gallery, Franchetti's most prized piece was Mantegna's *St Sebastian*. Also worth singling out is Tullio Lombardo's delightful marble double portrait. At the far end the *portego* provides fine views of the Grand Canal. Move on in time to the second floor where you can see fresco fragments by Giorgione and Titian – moved from the Fondaco dei Tedeschi for preservation.

The next palazzo, the **Ca' Rezzonico**, takes you into the 18th century. Though entire ceilings and many of the furnishings have been taken from other palaces it all looks very authentic and gives you some idea of what life was like in those hedonistic days. Six stops on the *vaporetto* (direction San Marco) will bring you to the Ca' Rezzonico landing stage. Just before the stop you can't miss the vast façade of the palace, with its columns, arcades, balconies and abundance of sculptural detail. To get there from the landing stage, take the Calle dei Traghetto to the Campo Santa Barnaba. Stop if you like for coffee in the square, watch the local life and morning shoppers scurrying to the floating vegetable market. Cross the bridge nearest the church and turn immediately right for the *palazzo*, marked *Museo del Settecento Veneziano* (Museum of 18th century Venice).

The palace was designed in 1667 by the only great Venetian baroque architect, Baldassare Longhena, and later bought by the fabulously rich Rezzonico family. At one time it was owned by

Robert Browning's reprobate son, Pen, and his wealthy American heiress wife – and it was while Robert Browning was staying here with them that he died of bronchitis. The interior of the palace is suitably grandiose. A formidable stone stairway leads up to the splendid ballroom with massive gilt chandeliers and frescoed ceilings. Beyond are a series of stately rooms embellished by frescoed ceilings, ostentatious vase stands and lacquered furniture. From the balcony at the end there are fine views of the Grand Canal.

The second floor is arranged as a picture gallery of 18th-century Venetian paintings. Don't miss the charming scenes by Longhi and the frolicsome paintings of carnival and clowns by Domenico Tiepolo. The third floor has a fascinating reconstruction of an 18th-century apothecary's shop and a puppet theatre.

If there is time and energy for another *palazzo*, opt for something entirely different: the eccentric **Palazzo Venier dei Leoni**, containing the Guggenheim Collection (closed Tuesdays). It is not far by foot from the Ca' Rezzonico; alternatively go one stop on the *vaporetto*, turn left when disembarking at *Accademia* and follow the signs. With its unfinished neoclassical façade (it is known as the Palazzo Nonfinito) the structure could look less like a Venetian *palazzo*. Peggy Guggenheim, the eccentric American art lover, bought the palace in 1949 and lived here until she died in 1979. Her collection is all 20th century, with the emphasis on Surrealism. The majority of the works came directly from the artists, whom she befriended, patronised, entertained or – in the case of Max Ernst – married. She is buried here behind the *palazzo* with her dogs.

Whether or not you visit the Guggenheim, the Dorsoduro is a good area to stay for lunch – either a snack on the Zattere or a full meal at one of three restaurants between the Guggenheim and the Accademia: the **Ai Gondolieri**, **Ai Cugnai** (see *Eating Out* for both) or the newly refurbished **Cantinone Storico**.

Palazzo Venier dei Leoni, housing the Guggenheim Collection

5. Torcello – Relic of Former Glory

Leave behind the splendour of La Serenissima for a tiny island on the lagoon. Lunch at a famous 'locanda' or a rustic trattoria, then visit the surviving sights of this once flourishing island.

It is hard to believe that the flat little island of Torcello, with a population of around 70, was once the centre of a thriving civilisation. In its heyday the population was around 20,000, but as Venice rose to power, decay set in. Trade dwindled, the waters silted up and malaria spread. Today, the cathedral, church and a couple of *palazzi* are the sole evidence of former splendour. It is a lonely, nostalgic and – if you are in the mood – very romantic island.

Take the No 12 ferry from Fondamente Nuove (see Itinerary 8, which takes the same route). The trip takes about 50 minutes, stopping en route at Murano, and sometimes Burano. Avoid Sunday in summer if you can. From afar you can spot the campanile of the cathedral above the flat marshland. From the landing stage follow the island's only 'road' – a rustic path beside a narrow canal. It all seems extraordinarily quiet and rural in comparison to the city.

If you lunch at the **Locanda Cipriani** you will be following in the footsteps of famous visitors such as Hemingway (who spent an entire winter here shooting duck in the lagoon and completing his book *Across the River and into the Trees*), Queen Elizabeth, Sir Winston Churchill, Charlie Chaplin and Sophia Loren. The Locanda, which has five bedrooms, is run by the sister of Arrigo Cipriani, owner of Harry's Bar. Like its par-

Torcello stallholder

ent establishment it prides itself on its home-made pastas, *carpaccio* (wafer thin slices of raw fillet of beef) and its *dolci*. Prices may be on the high side but the place itself is pleasantly unpretentious and quiet; on a warm day you can sit on the terrace overlooking gardens, church and cathedral. Cheaper alternatives are the pleasantly rural **Ponte del Diavolo** (on the left before you get to the centre) and the **Villa 600**, close to the cathedral.

After lunch spare a moment for the old ladies selling lace and linen at open-air stalls, then start sightseeing where the settlement began: the **Cathedral of Santa Maria Assunta** (open 2pm, admission charge). This was started as early as AD639 but rebuilt between the 9th and 11th centuries. Note the foundations of the original baptistry on your left and before you go in, the massive stone slabs acting as shutters on the south side of the cathedral, dating from the 11th century. The interior – simple, spacious, light and dignified – is immensively impressive and its mosaics are among the oldest and finest in Italy. Most striking of all is *The Virgin and Child*, set against a glowing gold background in the dome of the central apse. To the right the mosaic of *Christ in Benediction with Saints and Angels* dates from the same century and is based on a design from mosaics in San Vitale church, Ravenna.

Covering the entire western wall is *The Last Judgement*, a massive, elaborate mosaic full of narrative. From this end admire the church in its entirety: the slender marble columns, the wooden tie-beams, and the roodscreen carved with peacocks, lions and flowers, surmounted by a frieze of 15th-century paintings. The 11th century pavement is impressive too, and between the 6th and 7th columns a wooden flap reveals part of the original floor.

The church of **San Fosca**, adjoining the cathedral via a pretty portico, was built in the 11th century to enshrine the body of Santa Fosca, the Christian martyr. Close to the church, the primitive stone chair, known as *Attila's Seat*, was once said to have been used by the king of the Huns. A more likely theory is that it was used by the island tribunes. According to local folklore if you sit on the chair you will be married within the year.

On the opposite side of the piazza to the cathedral and church, the *Palazzo dell'Archivio and Palazzo del Consiglio* have been restored to house the **Museo dell'Estuario (Museum of the Lagoon)** (closed Monday). Here you'll find a collection of archaeological finds from the the earliest days of Torcello's history. The ferries back to Venice go about every hour – you can get a timetable from the Locanda Cipriani. Some boats go back via Burano, in which case you may like to spend an hour or so here before the return trip to Venice (see Itinerary 7).

6. A Boat to Burano

Burano is the most colourful of the islands in the lagoon. The waterways are bordered by brightly coloured houses, streets are lined with lace and linen stalls and the fishing and boatbuilding communities are very much in evidence. Spend the afternoon here, relaxing perhaps after a morning's serious sightseeing in Venice – or combine it with a trip to Torcello and/or Murano.

Boats for Burano leave from the Fondamenta Nuove roughly every hour and take 40–50 minutes. Ask for details at your hotel or in the tourist office. Avoid summer weekends when the boats are packed to capacity. If you choose to go to the island in time for lunch, there are plenty of very pleasant open-air *trattorias* specialising in fish. Ferries for Burano depart from the landing stage by the bridge near the Gesuiti church. Arrive in good time to get a seat on the upper deck. Tickets can be bought on board. Sit on the right hand side for the best views of the islands of the lagoon.

The first you pass is the cemetery island of **San Michele** where several illustrious former visitors to Venice are buried. The boat will stop at **Murano**, centre of the Venetian glass-making industry since the end of the 13th century. Spot the *fornaci* (furnaces) as you go by. From here the ferry will head out into the lagoon for the more remote islands, passing through a channel delineated by piles where seagulls perch. On your right for most of the journey you

Typical scene on Burano, the most colourful of the lagoon's islands

The brightly-painted Casa Bepi

can see the marshy islets and main island of **Sant'Erasmo**, where fruit and vegetables are grown for Venetian consumption. To the left, in the distance, planes will be taking off and landing at Marco Polo airport. The ferry swings left around the deserted island of San Giacomo in Palude, one of many islands abandoned in the 1960s. To the right, in the distance a dark cluster of cypresses marks the island of San Francesco del Deserto.

As you get closer to Burano you will see its acutely leaning campanile. The ferry soon enters the canal of **Mazzorbo**, lined on the right by pink houses and gardens. The boat may go via Torcello which will take an extra 10 minutes. From afar you can see the campanile of the cathedral, towering above this tiny island. If you are stopping off here before Burano consult Itinerary 5. Burano strikes you as lively and colourful after a trip through the desolate lagoon. About 5,000 people live here, many of them fishermen or glass workers who commute to the factories of Murano. Take away the canals and it looks and feels something like a Greek island.

From the landing stage follow the general flow past souvenir stalls and painted houses where you may see ladies busily embroidering at the front doors. Explore the island at leisure – it is small enough to do so. If you are planning to eat, do so in the Via Baldassare Galuppi, the main street of the island, named after the composer who was born here. The restaurant with the best reputation (and hence the highest prices) is an ex-haunt of artists, the **Trattoria da Romano** (closed Tuesday) on the left at No 221. Stick to fish – either as *antipasto*, in soup or freshly grilled – and you are unlikely to be disappointed.

To view the most colourful *cortile* (courtyard) on the island, take the tiny alley opposite the Galuppi restaurant in the same street. Casa Bepi at No 339 has a multicoloured geometrical façade which truly dazzles the eye. The ubiquitious **lace and linen** stalls and

Burano lace – beware of imitations

shops all vie for attention. There are some reasonable purchases to be had among the tablecloths, napkins and blouses, but don't be fooled into thinking it is all handmade on Burano. Much of it is factory made in Asia and the prices on the island are more or less the same as those in Venice itself. In the 16th-century, Venetian, and particularly Burano, lace was in great demand. So much so that the court of Louis XIV closed its doors to lace from Venice and created a royal industry of its own. Every means possible was used to steal the industry from the *Serenissima*, by inducing women to leave Burano and providing them with workshops where new designs – though clearly Venetian in influence – were invented.

The downfall of the Republic of Venice led to the inevitable decline of the industry, but an important revival took place in 1872 when a lacemaking school was founded in an effort to combat local poverty. Today Burano is one of the last surviving centres of handmade lace. To see authentic Burano lace and the ladies who make it, pay a visit to the **Scuola dei Merletti** in the Piazza Baldassare Galuppi. Here priceless antique pieces are displayed behind glass and upstairs the women busily stitch away in the old tradition.

The late afternoon, when most of the tourists have left the island, is the best time to be in Burano. Siesta time is over and the *Buranelli*, as the locals are called, are out painting their boats or mending nets. Ferries leave for Venice every hour or so until late at night. At dusk, when the sun is setting over the lagoon, is a beautiful time to return.

Portrait in glass of Garibaldi

7. Murano – A Galaxy of Glass

Discover the island of Murano, where glass has been made for centuries. Watch the blowing, see the showrooms and visit the world's finest collection of Venetian glass.

The island of Murano is sometimes described as a mini-Venice. It cannot match the city for splendour but, like Venice, it is made up of islands and divided by canals which are lined by old mansions and *palazzi*. It even has its own Grand Canal. But unlike Venice, Murano's *raison d'être* is – and has been for centuries – the making of glass.

As early as the 7th century a glass industry was established near Venice. In the late 13th century the factories were moved to Murano to avoid the hazards of fire from the open furnaces. The Murano glass-makers enjoyed rare privileges. But their craft was a closely guarded secret and they left the shores of Venice on penalty of death. Even so, many of the glassmakers were lured abroad in the 16th century. Those who were discovered, including a few who divulged their secrets to the court of Louis XIV, were condemned to death. About 60 per cent of the glass produced today is exported. Shops sell everything from glass bonbons and gondolas to priceless chandeliers. The characteristics of the local glass are bright colour and ornate design.

Beware of free trips to Murano, offered by touts milling in Piazza San Marco. For each tourist brought to the relevant show-

Murano

Chair inlaid with blue glass in the Glass Museum

room, the tout is paid a hefty commission. Hence very heavy pressure to buy and prices which are often more than those in Venice. To go independently, take the No 5 *vaporetto* (*circolare sinistra*) from the San Zaccaria landing stage near San Marco. This takes you through the Arsenale and across to Murano via the island of San Michele.

To avoid the pressure from smooth-operating glass vendors, wait until the fourth stop on the island (Museo) before you get off. Signs will lead you to the **Museo Vetrario** (Glass Museum) on the Fondamenta Giustinian, keep your ticket for the Museum of Modern Glass. Pieces are well displayed behind glass but most of the descriptions are only in Italian. Concentrate on the Roman exhibits on the ground floor and the 15th and 16th-century pieces on the first floor in the room to the left, many of them richly coloured and highly decorated. A prize piece is the *Coppa Barovier* (Barovier being one of a dynasty of Muranese glassmakers) – a 15th-century wedding cup in dark blue glass with enamelwork decoration.

Leaving the museum, turn left and follow the canal for the beautiful Veneto-Byzantine **Basilica SS Maria e Donato**. Admire the apse with its double-tier of arches and dog-tooth and zigzag patterns; then, if it is open, go inside to see the ship's keel roof, fine mosaic floor, marble columned Byzantine-style arcades and mosaic of the Virgin over the apse.

Retrace your steps back to the Museo landing stage, follow the Fondamenta along the Canal Grande and cross the Ponte Vivarini – named after the 15th-century family of painters who lived on Murano. From the bridge you can see the **Palazzo da Mula** (on the

Glass furnace

far bank to your right), one of Murano's few surviving grand mansions. At the far side of the bridge, turn left along the Rio dei Vetrai for the church of **San Pietro Martire**, which contains two great altarpieces by Giovanni Bellini.

Further along, the Fondamenta is more or less given over to glass factories, glass shops and glass showrooms. Many pieces in the shops are from the Far East and it is difficult to tell what is made in Murano and what is not. On the other side of the canal visit the **Museum of 20th-Century Murano Glass** to see some stylish contemporary pieces. And if you haven't seen a glass-blowing display, stop at one of the workshops. With incredible skill the craftsman blows the heated glass paste into the desired form, then with a spatula and pair of pincers, twists, turns, pinches and flattens it into a perfect shape.

The landing stage for boats back to Venice lies at the end of the Rio dei Vetrai. Boats going to Torcello and Burano (see Itineraries 5 and 7) stop at the Faro landing stage east of the *rio*.

8. Beach Break at the Lido

Leave the sights of the city, catch a 'vaporetto' to Venice's main bathing resort and cool off in the waters of the Adriatic. Avoid summer Sundays when all Venetians go.

The 11km (6 ¾ mile) strip of land protecting the Venetian lagoon from the Adriatic was Italy's first *lido*. Nineteenth-century romantics came here to escape the city, to walk or ride along the sands and swim. By the turn of the 20th century it was one of the most fashionable resorts of Europe and the name was subsequently applied to dozens of bathing resorts throughout the world. The Lido may have lost some of its cachet since the days of Visconti's film *Death in Venice*, but the beach still provides an essential cooling-off experience on a scorching hot day. If you are with children, a trip here will be top priority. The ferry ride across the lagoon, which only takes 12 or 20 minutes (depending on which boat you take) is fun in itself.

Unless you are sufficiently affluent to go by gondola or motor launch you will take a No 1, 2, 6 or 34 boat from the Riva degli

Hôtel des Bains

Schiavoni (l, 2 and 34 also go from the Piazzale Roma), No 6 being direct. Public boats link the Lido to the city, leaving on average every four minutes. If you want to try your luck at the casino, which opens at 3pm, remember to take your passport for identification and line your pockets with plenty of *lire*.

You arrive on the Lido at the Piazzale Santa Maria Elisabetta. From here take the Gran Viale Santa Maria Elisabetta, the main road leading to the beaches. Cars, buses and taxis with wheels come as something of a shock if you have already acclimatised yourself to the traffic-free streets of Venice.

Follow the street to the far end where you can look over the beach from the Piazzale Bucintoro. Turn right for the **Lungomare G Marconi**, the boulevard boasting the best hotels and beaches. The only public beaches are the strips either end which, being free, are inevitably the least desirable. You can treat yourself to a beach hut with comfortable sunbeds provided by hotels which have concessions on the beach, but these do not come cheap. You cannot do much better than the beach opposite the **Grand Hôtel des Bains**, where the sand is manicured daily. Otherwise keep to the sand nearest to the water's edge, where no one can turf you off. Recent surveys have evidently found the waters at the Lido to be among the cleanest along the Adriatic coast. Judge for yourself.

The **Hôtel des Bains** is the Lido's most famous landmark, immortalized by Thomas Mann and Luchino Visconti (*Death in Venice* was filmed here). Further along, the **Palazzo del Casinò** and **Palazzo del Cinema**, where the International Film Festival is held every summer, are typical of the architecture of the Fascist 1930s. Another familiar landmark, the **Excelsior Hotel** is an exuberant piece of neo-Byzantine architecture built at the turn of the century.

Beach life

The Lido is Venice's main centre for sport. Ask at the Excelsior Hotel about tickets for non-residents at the Lido Venice Club, which offers a variety of watersports, riding, tennis and golf. If you would rather take to the skies, the *Aeroclub di Venezia* at San Nicolò airport in the north of the island, offers hour-long flights over Venice.

Try and time your return trip to Venice as the sun is setting. The approach to San Marco, via the island of San Giorgio Maggiore, is an experience you are unlikely to forget.

Sunset return to the Serenissima

Shopping

9. Afternoon Delights

Dig deep into your wallet or content yourself with a feast of window-fronts. All the great names of Italian high fashion are here and, if you are looking for something more local, Venetian craftsmanship continues to flourish despite the influx of imitations from the East.

You don't have to look far to find fascinating small specialist shops and local artisans at work in their ateliers. Watch out for beautifully crafted Venetian masks, marbled paper, Murano glass, handmade picture frames, lace, linen and costume jewellery.

'The most delicious streete in the world' was how John Evelyn described the **Mercerie** in 1645. It was the main street of Venice, its shops filled with sumptuous goods from the east: golden cloth and rich damask, tapestries and carpets, perfumes, potions and spices.

Crafts and souvenirs

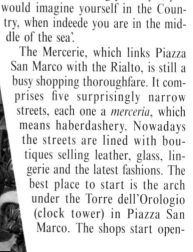

Caged nightingales sang sweet melodies and the streets were free of rattling coaches, 'so as shutting your Eyes, you would imagine yourself in the Country, when indeede you are in the middle of the sea'.

The Mercerie, which links Piazza San Marco with the Rialto, is still a busy shopping thoroughfare. It comprises five surprisingly narrow streets, each one a *merceria*, which means haberdashery. Nowadays the streets are lined with boutiques selling leather, glass, lingerie and the latest fashions. The best place to start is the arch under the Torre dell'Orologio (clock tower) in Piazza San Marco. The shops start open-

Miniature glass baroque orchestra

ing at 3–3.30pm. If you are
low on *lire*, change cash or traveller's cheques either at CIT or
Thomas Cook on the square
(both open at 3pm) or, to avoid
hefty commission charges, at
the Banco di Roma, Merceria
dell'Orologio 191.

There are about six times as many shoes in Venice as there are
Venetians and you will see a good proportion of them along the
Mercerie, starting with the stylish but affordable **Zecchi** on your
right. To see authentic Venetian crafts visit **Veneziartigiana**, at
412–13 Calle Larga San Marco, the first street on your right. This
is a fine old apothecary shop converted into a showroom for crafts
designed in glass, silver, bronze, china, lace and gold. Further
along the street turn right and almost immediately left. Across the
bridge you can watch glassblowing; to your right, over the Ponte
Canonica, you will see the entrance to **Jesurum**, an old and beautiful *scuola* housing the finest lace and linen.

Return now to the Mercerie and work your way north along the
narrow streets following signs for the Rialto. **Galvin** at Merceria
dell'Orologio No 229 has a large range of top-quality handmade
gloves. Opposite, **Pagnacco**'s windowfront shows a miniature
baroque orchestra in Murano glass and miniscule glass insects.
Continue to the top of the Mercerie, past more shoes, jewellers,
boutiques and glass shops. At No 4983 **Renè** has some exception-
ally elegant shoes, including star-studded stilettoes.

At the Campo San Salvador divert briefly from the route to the
Rialto by turning left into the Calle dei Lovo. Here you will find a
shop selling luscious-looking chocolates and sweets and a *pasticce-*

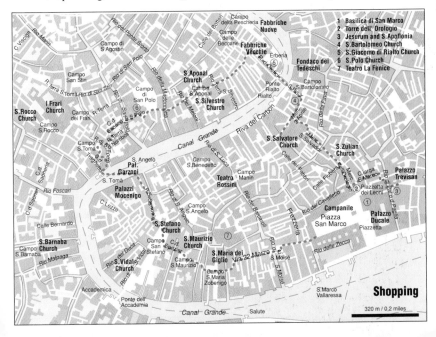

Rialto view

ria with elaborate cakes, marzipan shapes, croissants and brioches. If you feel like coffee and a cake here's the place to stop.

Return to Campo San Salvador and go straight on into the Campo San Bartolomeo. Turn immediately left for the **Rialto Bridge**. Squeeze past the tourists and the trash and make the most of the bird's eye views of the Grand Canal. Then come down into the Ruga degli Orefici, street of the gold-smiths, where jewellers have hung out for centuries. Best buys in

the Rialto area are silk ties, soft leather wallets, lambs wool and angora sweaters.

Turn left into the Ruga Vecchia San Giovanni, and follow the main flow going in the Piazzale Roma direction. Catch wafts of homemade bread as you pass food shops and *trattorias*. Carry on past a variety of shops into the busy Campo San Aponal. Cross the square, following the signs for the Piazzale Roma, into a tiny alley where a shop on the right sells miniature silver gondolas, tortoises and frogs. Carry on to the lovely Campo di San Polo where children will be out playing. Follow the signs for the Piazzale Roma, go straight on into Calle Saoneri, with some fascinating specialist shops. At **Amadi Bruni**, No 2747, you may see a craftsman at work making tiny glass mice or spiders. Turning left at the end you will pass a shop with a large choice of prints of Venice. In the Calle dei Nomboli which follows, the exotic masks at **Tragicomica** are sure to catch your eye.

Just before you come into the Campo San Tomà, follow the yellow sign for the *traghetto*. If you haven't been on a gondola now is the time to do so. These ferry services cross the canal at half a dozen points. Step on board, pay the small fee and trust the gondolier to weave his way deftly through the traffic along the Grand Canal. Once off the boat take the narrow street ahead, then walk to the end of the Piscina San Samuele. Take a left turn into Calle degli Botteghe which will bring you face to face with the church of San Stefano. Turn right into the square and take the narrow street marked to San Marco.

On your way back to Piazza San Marco you will be

Antiques in Campo San Stefano

Marbled paper

passing some of the smartest shops in the city. In the Calle del Spezier you may well be delayed by the **Pasticceria Marchini** which has an irresistable selection of cakes, pastries and multicoloured chocolate. In Campo Maurizio two shops sell exotic fabrics, some with Fortuny designs. **BAC art studio** specialises in prints, posters and hand-painted frames.

In Campiello della Feltrina, **Legatoria Piazzesi** has a wonderful selection of hand-printed paper, with distinctive marble designs. You can see the antique woodblocks which are still used to make them by the traditional *carta varese* method. There is plenty of scope for gifts here: decorative boxes, frames, albums, sketch books and card games.

In Calle dei Ostreghe the trendy and high-priced **Krizia** has some eyecatching fashions. The **Calle Larga XXII Marzo** and the streets between here and Piazza San Marco are the smartest shopping addresses in town. The **Salizzada San Moisè** boasts big names in shoes, bags and fashions. Try **Osvaldo Böhm** for prints, etchings and watercolours of Venice. In Calle Vallaressa on the right before you get to Piazza San Marco, **Camiceria San Marco** will make you shirts and pyjamas within 24 hours. Slightly more off-beat and fun is the street called **Frezzeria** running north of the Salizzada San Moisè. A fitting end to the day is **Piazza San Marco** whose arcades shelter luxury jewellers, hand-embroidered linen and lace and priceless pieces of glass.

Street artists are not always flattering

Eating

Despite their past trade in exotic spices and foods, Venetians never seem to have really excelled gastronomically. The mainstay of their diet has nearly always been fish fresh from the lagoon and rice from the Po valley. Venetian specialities are limited and hardly adventurous. Those you find most frequently are *risi e bisi* (rice and peas cooked with onion, ham and herbs in a chicken stock), *pasta e fagioli* (pasta and bean soup) and *fegato alla veneziana* (thinly sliced calves' liver with sauté onions and slabs of grilled *polenta*). The mediocrity of much Venetian cui-

sine, coupled with high costs, often leads to disappointment when it comes to dining out.

There are, of course, exceptions and sufficient of them to keep the brief visitor satisfied. The restaurants in the itineraries have been handpicked for excellence of quality and (by Venetian standards) value. Listed overleaf are several more, starting with the well-known gastronomic venues where you pay an arm and a leg for the very best, to off-the-beaten-track cheap family-run trattorias and cafés. The simple rule to avoid the highest prices – whether it's a cup of coffee or a five-course blow-out – is to steer clear of San Marco. To avoid all the hidden extras such as cover charge (L2,000-L5,000) and service (12% or more) opt for the set menus. These start at around L20,000 for a three-course inclusive meal. The cheapest eating tends to be in the north of the city, in and around Cannaregio or the San Giacomo dall'Orio area in Santa Croce. Often an *antipasto* followed by a pasta or rice dish (eg *prosciutto* and melon, followed by fish risotto) is more enjoyable and works out cheaper than a main meat or fish course.

Fish features on virtually every menu; if you are lucky it will be that morning's catch. Most of the fish, either displayed outside restaurants or at the Rialto fish market, is caught a long way from the lagoon and prices are far from reasonable. A seafood antipasto (*antipasto di mare*) could put you back L18,000 lire and a plate of grilled mixed fish (*grigliata mista di pesce*) L20,000 to L25,000. Among the fish and seafood you are likely to come across are sole, sea bass, turbot, mullet, San Pietro (a tasty white fish), crayfish, crab, cuttle fish and squid. Also worth trying are *granseoli*, sea spiders from Yugoslavia, served cold with lemon and olive oil; or *moleche*, small crabs caught as they are changing their shells, fried with oil, garlic and herbs. You can eat the shell and pincers too.

Pasta comes in all sizes and colours. Try the local speciality, *bigoli* – black strands of spaghetti made with wholewheat flour, served perhaps with an anchovy or tuna sauce. Practically any pasta served with seafood is a safe bet. Look out for pastas *alla vongole* (with clams), *ai frutti di mare* (with shell fish) or *alla marinara* (with mixed seafood). The favourite dessert is *tiramisù* (literally 'pick-me-up') – a creamy alcoholic coffee and chocolate gâteau.

Wine

The house wine, *vino della casa*, is usually perfectly drinkable, often very pleasant. It is likely to be a dry white Tocai or a dry Cabernet or Merlot (reds), all from the Friuli region to the north of Venice. In the cheaper establishments wine will be served in litre or half-litre carafes or jugs. You are also bound to come across the familiar names from the Veneto: Valpolicella, Bardolino and Soave.

As an aperitif there is little to beat a glass of Prosecco or Cartizzi, good quality sparkling white wines from the Veneto. Many Venetians drink them with their meals.

Expensive Restaurants

L90,000–L150,000

For setting, there is little to beat the top-floor restaurant of the Danieli Hotel and the terrace of the Gritti Palace, overlooking the Grand Canal. At all the restaurants listed it is wise to make reservations in advance.

ANTICO MARTINI
Campo San Fantin 1983.
Tel: 522 4121.
Closed Tuesday and Wednesday.
Save this one for a celebration. Cuisine (international and classic Italian) is among the best in Venice, charming setting, elegant clientele.

HARRY'S BAR
Calle Vallaresso 1323.
Tel: 528 5777.
Closed Monday and
January to mid-February.
A Venetian institution, run by Harry (Arrigo) Cipriani and full of Americans trying to spot celebrities. Cuisine

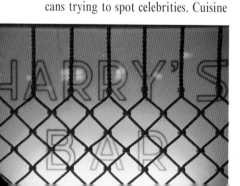

is still considered the best in Venice, particularly pasta. Speciality is *carpaccio* which Hemingway used to enjoy here. Cheapest meal is the set lunch at around L80,000 without wine.

TAVERNA LA FENICE
Campiello de la Fenice,
San Marco 1938.
Tel: 522 3856.
Closed Wednesday.
Elegant dining room and large terrace, close to the Fenice theatre. Popular among the more affluent performers at the Fenice.

Moderate Restaurants

L40,000–L80,000

ALTANELLA
Calle dell'Erbe, Giudecca 268.
Tel: 522 7780.
Closed Monday, Tuesday and winter.
Friendly family run trattoria with excellent fish dishes. Terrace overlooking canal. Reservations advisable.

ANTICA BESSETA
Santa Croce 1395
(near San Giacomo dell'Orio).
Tel: 721 687.
Closed Tuesday and Wednesday.
Hard to find but worth the effort for fresh fish and scarcity of tourists.

Da Arturo

Calle degli Assassini, San Marco 3656.
Tel: 528 6974.
Closed Sunday, holidays and three weeks in August.

Small and unique in that it serves no fish. Imaginative salads and pastas, first class fillet steak. End the meal with *tirami sù*. Close to the Fenice – reserve in advance if you want to eat after an opera or concert.

Cantinone Storico

Rio San Vio, Dorsoduro 660/661.
Tel: 523 9577.
Closed Wednesday.

Close to the Accademia and once a haunt of artists. Recently refurbished at grand expense. Prices now start at L40,000 for a meal.

Ai Cugnai

Dorsoduro 857.
Tel: 528 9238.
Closed Monday.

Busy trattoria run by three sisters, just two minutes from the Accademia. Small, quite homely, with wood-pannelling and pictures.

Da Fiore

Calle del Scaleter, San Polo 2202.
Tel: 721308.
Closed Sunday and Monday.

Inconspicuous, elegant and excellent for fish. Above average service. Mainly Venetian clientele.

Da Franz

Fondamenta S. Giuseppe, Castello 754.
Tel: 522 0861/522 7505.
Closed Tuesday and January.

Off the beaten track, close to the public gardens, excellent for seafood. Lots of Venetians. Only open for dinner except at weekends when lunch is also served.

La Furatola

Calle Lunga Santa Barnaba, Dorsoduro 2870A.
Tel: 520 8594.
Closed Wednesday pm, all Thursday, sometimes Monday (depending on the market), July and August.

One of the city's best-value fish restaurants where the produce is always fresh. Try the *moleche* (soft crabs), *spaghetti alle vongole* or *alle seppie nere* and watch what is cooking in the kitchen from your table. Desserts are homemade.

Ai Gondolieri

Fondamente Ospedaleto, Dorsodoro 366.
Tel: 528 6396.
Closed Wednesday.

Modern, with black and white 1950s photos on wood-pannelled walls. Dependable cuisine with emphasis on meat. The meal starts with a variety of breads which you dip in a pot of olive oil and mustard. The *antipasti della casa* is well worth trying.

Harry's Dolci

Giudecca 773
(close to Sant'Eufemia landing stage).
Tel:520 8337.
Closed Tuesday and Wednesday and November to mid March.

Offshoot of Harry's Bar with similar food at slightly cheaper prices and excellent cakes served all day. Outdoor terrace with lovely views over the Giudecca Canal.

Da Remigio
Salizzada dei Greci, Castello 3416.
Tel: 523 0089.
Closed Tuesday.
Excellent value for fish and seafood. A large, bustling trattoria, with plenty of locals. Usually packed.

Inexpensive Restaurants

L20,000–L25,000

Not surprisingly this is a short list.

Antico Molo
Fondamenta degli Ormesini,
Cannaregio, 2800.
Tel: 717492.
Closed Saturday.
Off the beaten track, this trattoria is

close to the ghetto. Not as simple as it used to be, nevertheless this is still a place to see the locals and try some typical Venetian cuisine.

Alla Pergola
Fondamenta della Sensa,
Cannaregio 3318a.
Tel: 720198.
Simple homely *osteria* with picturesque canalside setting in quiet area of Cannaregio. Good, basic meals are the speciality, with some of the least expensive prices in town.

Roma
Lista di Spagna, Cannaregio 122.
Tel: 716038.
Closed Friday.
Close to the railway station with reasonably priced set meals.

Rosa Rossa
Calle della Mandola, San Marco 3709.
Tel: 523 4605.
Closed Wednesday.
Pizzeria/trattoria situated in a busy alley of shops.

Wine Bars

Vino Vino
Ponte della Veste, San Marco 2007A.
Closed Tuesday.
Large selection of Italian (and other) wines served by the glass or bottle. Snacks and typical Venetian dishes.

Al Milion
Corte al Milion, Cannaregio 5841.
Closed Sunday and August.
Old wine tavern with large range of snacks and seafood. Be prepared to queue. It is hidden behind the church of S Giovanni (near the Rialto) in a courtyard, where Marco Polo's house is said to have stood. Try *pasta e fagioli*, fish soup or *carpaccio*.

Cafés and Snacks

To avoid service charge (exorbitant if you are sitting out on a ter-race), stand at a bar or café for *panini* (bread rolls with fillings), *tramezzini* (fat sandwiches, often with delicious fillings) or *cicheti* – savoury snacks, such as meat balls, baby squid, artichoke hearts, cheese or *prosciutto*, usually taken with wine. If you are feeling ad-venturous try *nervetti*, ox nerves boiled with onions, pepper and salt, then cut into small pieces. There are several self-service places with tables. *Pizzerias* can be surprisingly expensive by the time the cover charge and service charge have been added.

Venice has no shortage of cafés. The most elegant among them is Florian's in Piazza San Marco, a meeting place for Venetian soci-ety since 1720. Here a *cappuccino* will set you back L6,500; a salmon sandwich, which is only another L1,500, seems cheap at the price. If the orchestra is playing add another L3,500 to your order. The larger squares of the city have much cheaper open-air cafés and there are plenty of bars where Venetians like to take their pre-pran-dial *ombra* or glass of wine. *Pasticcerie* throughout the city have a tempting array of cakes, croissants, pastries and strudel – a legacy of the Austrian occupation.

Florian's café in Piazza San Marco

Nightlife

No-one comes to Venice for nightlife. The locals joke that it's so quiet you can see angels dancing on the roof of the Basilica after midnight. That does not mean you should retire after your evening meal. On the contrary, this is when you will be most aware of the magical qualities of the city. The crowds disappear, focal points are floodlit and gondolas glide silently along the canals. Venice is one of the safest cities in Europe, so relax as you take a late-night stroll through the city. It is a

Music in the piazza

lovely time to see the Piazza. Here on summer evenings café orchestras play, artists set up easels and occasionally it becomes a stage set for concerts, theatre or ballet.

The most pleasurable evening pursuit is to take to the canals in a gondola. This symbol of Venice has been carrying passengers and cargo for over 1,000 years. By the 16th century there were approximately 10,000 gondolas – now there are a mere 400. For grace and elegance there is nothing to rival the gondola. It is sleek and black, long and narrow, elegantly curved at either end and manoeuvred by a single oar. The gondolier stands at the rear, rowing and steering the boat with amazing dexterity and grace.

The 16th-century gondola was a brightly coloured, richly carved vessel and nobles used to vie with each other over the number they owned and the ornamentation their boats displayed. But sumptuary decrees in the 17th century forbade any sort of ostentation. All boats were to be painted black and the *felze*, the cabins providing passengers' anonymity and protection from the rain, were to be stripped of their lavish coverings. Only foreign ambassadors were exempt from the law. Since then all gondolas, other than those used during regattas, have been painted black – prompting allusions to mystery, melancholia and death. The vast majority of today's gondolas are only used by visitors. Wealthy Venetians own a motor launch, which is faster and cheaper to maintain.

It may not seem like it but charges for the gondola are officially regulated. Before your trip consult the free booklet *Un Ospite di Venezia* (available from main hotels and tourist office) for the current prices. These should also be prominently displayed in every gondola and are around L70,000 (the minimum charge) for 50 minutes, L35,000 for each 25 minutes thereafter and L20,000 extra if you travel after 8pm. Gondoliers are notorious for cheating unsuspecting tourists and it's essential to agree a fee before you start.

You may wish to choose your own route or leave it to the gondolier. My suggestion combines the classic panoramas of Venice with vistas along some of the quieter canals. Firstly find a gondolier from the landing stage outside Harry's Bar. By all means begin with a cocktail at Venice's famous bar, but for the price of a drink you can buy at least one bottle of Prosecco, a delightful slightly sparkling white wine. Equip yourself with a couple of glasses and a camera and you are ready. Ask for the following route, which will take around an hour and cost in the region of L100,000: Bridge of Sighs, Santa Maria Formosa and Rialto Bridge, returning via the Grand Canal. Like all gondoliers, yours will have undergone several years' apprenticeship before getting his licence and he will have taken basic exams in the history of Venice and its art. His English will suffice to tell you about the buildings you pass, other highlights on the way and even perhaps some juicy pieces of Venetian gossip.

You may not notice but the right half of the boat is slightly narrower than the left. This was an alteration made in the 1880s by Domenico Tramontin which creates the elegant swinging motion and increases the speed of the gondola. The *ferro* which you can see on the prow, looking like an elongated comb with six 'teeth', is said to symbolise the six *sestieri* or quarters of Venice. Enough words. Concentrate now on the ride. Sit back, sip your Prosecco and glide silently past some of the most glorious views of Venice.

Ask to be dropped at the restaurant **Da Raffaele**, Fondamenta delle Ostreghe, where you can step straight from your gondola to a table by the canal. To ensure a waterside seat make a reservation in advance: Tel: 5232317.

Sunset on the lagoon

Calendar of Special Events

The only off-peak season in Venice is mid-winter when low temperatures, grey skies and the risk of flooding put off tourists. Peaceful streets and wintry mists have romantic appeal but it can be just plain cold and foggy. Springtime can be surprisingly cool and there is no real guarantee of warm sunshine until May. The best months overall to be in Venice are May, June, September and October. The most crowded times are Carnival, Easter and mid-summer. Tourist offices can provide you with leaflets on the year's special events and a booklet with listings.

JANUARY–MARCH

The advantages of going in January to March are cheaper hotel prices and fewer tourists. Duckboards and gumboots come out when the signs go up or the sirens are sounded for the *acque alte*, high waters. This is a good time of year for opera lovers (the season lasts from November to May).

The winter peace is briefly disturbed by the **Carnival** two weeks before Lent. The 18th century was the great age of masked balls and carnivals, but all this came to an abrupt halt when the republic fell and Napoleon had all the masks burnt. Carnival was only revived in the late 1970s. It lasts for ten days, during which time masks are donned, fantasies and passions acted out and social divisions discarded. The whole city becomes a stage set for exotic costumes, parades, pageants and concerts, culminating on Shrove Tuesday, a huge masked ball in the Piazza and a firework display over the Bacino di San Marco. Anyone wanting a room should resere several months ahead. Masks and costumes can be hired in Venice.

Carnival

JULY–SEPTEMBER

These are the months to avoid, when the city at its hottest and most crowded. Main event is the **Festa del Redentore**, when a bridge of boats is built across the Giudecca Canal to the Redentore – the church which was built in gratitude for deliverance of the city from the plague of 1576. The festival is one of the most colourful events of the city with hundreds of people rowing out to picnic on the water. The event ends with a firework display and crowds rowing out to the Lido to watch the sun rise.

Late August/early September is celebrity-spotting time on the Lido, venue for the **International Film Festival** which lasts for two weeks.

On the first Sunday in September the **Regata Storica** (historic regatta) opens with a spectacular procession of traditional boats on the Grand Canal, with rowers in costume.

NOVEMBER

The opera season starts at the Fenice theatre, the main festival is the **Festa della Madonna della Salute (21st)**. The church of Maria della Salute was also built in thanksgiving for the city's escape from a plague – this one, in 1630, took around 40,000 lives. The festival is centuries old and centres around a pontoon bridge built across the Grand Canal to the church.

APRIL

April sees the arrival of the package tourists. Temperatures can be surprisingly low and there is a risk of rain. **St Mark's Day** (25th), is when the gondoliers hold a race between Sant' Elena and the Punta della Dogana and traditionally everyone eats *risi e bisi* (rice and peas).

MAY

Spring generally is a good time for concerts at the Fenice and in the city's churches. Favourite event of the season and probably the year is the **Vogalonga**, held on the Sunday after Ascension Day. The word literally means 'long row' and the event involves hundreds of rowing boats following a course to Burano and back – about 32km (20 miles) along a designated course. Anyone with an oar-powered craft is welcome to take part. The race has its origins in the days when the doge would row out to the Lido in his ornate *Bucintoro* and ceremonially cast a ring into the water, symbolizing the marriage of Venice to the sea.

JUNE

In even-numbered years, June sees the start of the **Biennale Contemporary Art Exhibition**. It is held in permanent pavilions in the public gardens and the exhibitions go on until September/October. Exhibitions are also held in the Arsenale, at the old salt warehouses on the Zattere and at other venues in the city.

Practical Information

Visas

Visitors from the USA, EC and Commonwealth countries only need a passport for a stay of up to three months. Citizens of other countries should check with the nearest Italian consulate about obtaining a visa in advance of travel.

Getting There

From Marco Polo airport, 9km (5½ miles) north of Venice, the most appropriate and dramatic entry to Venice is by water. Avoid watertaxi touts and make sure you get the Cooperativa San Marco water launch which has an office inside the airport. It will take you across the lagoon, via the Lido and drop you at the waterfront by San Marco. The trip takes around 45 minutes. Going on a private watertaxi is quicker but costs six times as much. The alternative is to go by land. To the city terminal at Piazzale Roma, the coach takes 30 minutes, a land taxi takes 20–25 minutes.

Unless your hotel is very close to your arrival point you will have to take an exorbitantly priced watertaxi, struggle with your suitcases on foot or work out the waterbus system. Official porters can help but are hard to find.

Arriving by train you have the advantage of an information office within the station, more porters available and a wide choice of water transport below the station. On the minus side your introduction to the city of Venice is via the industrial complex of Mestre.

Arriving by car is best avoided.

Road route into the city

Garaging costs are high and space at Piazzale Roma for most of the year is non-existent. This means parking outside Venice, either at Tronchetto (a parking island) or Fusina found at the mouth of the Brenta Canal.

Time

Italy is six hours ahead of US Eastern Standard time and one hour ahead of Greenwich Mean Time.

National Holidays

The following are **national holidays** when banks, offices and many shops are shut: 1 January; Easter Monday; 25 April (Liberation Day); 1 May (Labour Day); 15 August (Assumption); 1 November (All Saints' Day); 8 December (Immaculate Conception); 25 and 26 December.

Electricity

Mains supply is 220v. Take an adaptor for electrical gadgets or buy one on the spot.

MONEY MATTERS

The basic unit of currency is the lira (L). Coins come in denominations of 50, 100, 200 and 500 lire; banknotes in 1,000, 2,000, 5,000, 10,000, 20,000, 50,000 and 100,000 lire.

Bank hours vary but are generally Monday–Friday 8.30am–1.30pm and 2.30pm–3.30pm. The bank at the railway station is open every day from 8.00am–7pm. The *bureaux de change* are open every day during shopping hours.

Bank rates vary but are usually the most favourable. *Bureaux de change*

Outside the railway station

charge a commission for each transaction, however small the amount.

Tipping

In restaurants service is normally included but it is normal to leave a little extra if the service deserves it. Hotel bills always include service but tip the porter for carrying your bags. Custodians in churches who light paintings or pinpoint masterpieces for you will appreciate a tip – or at least something for the church.

GETTING AROUND

Venice is surprisingly small. Going from north to south on foot takes only half an hour – if you happen to know the city well. First-time visitors always get lost. The most comprehen-

sive, accurate (and expensive) map is the *Touring Club Italiano*, not easily available outside Italy. The *Hallwag City Map 1:5500*, widely available in Venice and abroad, is one of the easiest maps to follow. Less detailed but quite useful is the free map from the tourist office. Wherever you are in Venice you are rarely far from the invaluable yellow signs which point the way to major landmarks: San Marco, Rialto, Ferrovia (railway station) and Piazzale Roma. The Grand Canal, sweeping through the heart of the city provides another vital landmark.

Waterbuses

The waterbus network is excellent, providing reasonably priced trips through and around the city. Best value for money is Line 1, the *accelarato*, which travels the length of the Grand Canal stopping at every landing stage. Line 2, a *motoscafo*, provides a faster service between the station and San Marco. Line 4, the *Turistico,* is a summer service along the Grand Canal and across to the Lido with few stops. Line 5, the *Circolare*, skirts the periphery of Venice in both directions and takes in the island of Murano. Line 34 is an *espresso* service from Tronchetto to San Marco going via the Grand Canal. Other boats provide a service to the Lido and islands. In high season boats along the main routes are packed.

The system is simple to follow provided your map shows the routes and you get on the right boat going in the right direction. Note the destinations signed on landing stages and if you are not sure ask the member of crew who helps passengers on and off the boat – they all have certificates in courtesy.

Tickets are available from most landing stages, some bars, tobacconists and shops displaying the ACTV sign. For the one ticket you can stay on the boat for as long as you like. Children under 1m (3ft) tall go free, but a suitcase costs as much as an ordinary passenger. Books of 10 or 20 tickets are available but at no saving. A ticket entitling you to unlimited journeys for 24 hours on all lines, except for No 2, is available, as is a three-day ticket. Well worth considering, even if you are only staying a few days is the *Carta Venezia*. It lasts for three years and is available from ACTV offices just off the San Angelo landing stage (Grand Canal) on presentation of a passport photograph.

Gondolas

Gondoliers may take you for a ride in both senses of the word (see *Nightlife*) so check the tariff and agree the fare first. At quiet times of day try bargaining. Ask at any travel agent for information regarding serenaded gondola 'groups'. The cheapest gondola is the *traghetto*, a ferry crossing the Grand Canal in six different places.

Water Taxis

These smart, varnished launches take up to four people. All of them have meters and must display a list of charges and a map of the city. You can find taxi 'ranks' at main points in the city, otherwise call 522 3326 or 522 2303.

Addresses

If you don't know the system, finding an address in Venice can be extremely tricky. Buildings are numbered not by the streets but by the administrative areas of the city. For example in the *Sestiere* of San Marco, the numbering starts with the Doge's Palace (No 1), works its way round the quar-

The main post office

ter and ends up at the Rialto. The address is simply the *sestiere* and the number, eg Castello 3348. If you are taking note of an address in Venice ask for a landmark or name of a street to help you get there.

Many streets, squares or churches are written in different ways, sometimes in Italian, sometimes in Venetian dialect. A name marked on a street or square may not always correspond to that given on a map or in the itineraries. Note the following before you start exploring the city.

calle	street
campo	square
campiello	small square
rio	canal
fondamenta	street along a canal
salizzada	paved street
ponte	bridge
sottportico/	
sotoportego	covered passageway
corte, cortile	courtyard

POST & TELECOMMUNICATION

The main Post Office, close to the Rialto Bridge in the Fondaco dei Tedeschi, is worth a visit for the fine courtyard. It is open Monday–Saturday 9am–8pm; Sunday 9am– noon. Other post offices, including one just west of Piazza San Marco in the Calle Larga del Ascensione, are open Monday–Friday 8.30am–1.30pm. Stamps can be bought in bars and tobacconists displaying a white 'T'. Mail sent from Italy is notoriously slow. If there is any urgency use the express delivery service.

Telegrams can be sent from the telegram office (open 24 hours) at the main post office at which a fax service is also available. Use Italcable for telegrams abroad; Tel: 186.

Public telephones are plentiful and the majority now take phone cards, available from tobacconists and newsstands. Public telephones also take coins though some of the older ones only accept *gettoni* (tokens). Long-distance calls can be made either from the ASST telephone office in Campo San Bartolomeo (near the Rialto Bridge) or from any call box. Telephoning from your hotel will cost considerably more. Cheapest time to call abroad is after 10pm, from 1pm on Saturday and all day Sunday.

HEALTH & EMERGENCIES

Venice is one of the safest cities in Europe but you should nevertheless watch your valuables in crowded places, especially on the *vaporetti*. It is best to leave valuables in the hotel safe and carry money on you rather than in a shoulderbag or handbag.

In the case of theft head immediately to the police (*Carabinieri*) to make an official declaration. A lost passport should be reported to your consulate.

General Emergency
Tel: 113

Police
Fondamenta San Lorenzo,
Castello 5053
Tel: 520 3222

Fire Brigade
Tel: 522 2222

Hospitals
Twenty-four hour casualty department at Ospedale Civile, Campo dei SS Giovanni e Paolo, Tel: 529 4111

Pharmacies
Local newspapers and the booklet *Un Ospite di Venezia* list late-night pharmacies. A late-night rota is also shown on the door of every pharmacy.

ACCOMMODATION

Most of the itineraries assume you are staying within easy reach of San Marco where most of the hotels are concentrated. The main alternative is the station area – not nearly as appealing, but cheaper and convenient if you are arriving by train or car and only staying a night or two.

Hotels in Venice are notoriously expensive. The top hotels are amongst the most expensive in the world and a simple central hotel costs roughly the same as a three-star hotel elsewhere in Italy. As a rule the closer you are to Piazza San Marco the higher the price, but you don't have to move very far away from the square before the cost starts to drop. One of the most pleasant areas to stay in is the Dorsoduro (see Day 2), a couple of

waterbus stops from San Marco or ten minutes by foot. Here there are several small, quiet and comparatively cheap hotels and *pensioni*.

Seasonal price variations are enormous. Go in winter to one of the top hotels and you will pay two-thirds – or in some cases even half – the peak-season rates. Prices are also very dependent on the size and outlook of the room. Look out onto the Grand Canal, rather than a brick wall or inner courtyard, and you will be paying dearly for the privilege.

Hidden extras to watch for are the expensive, unexceptional breakfasts, which by law should be 'optional' but which are almost invariably included in the room rate, air conditioning which can be as much as 10 per cent of the price of the room and IVA (VAT) of up to 19 per cent which is not always included in the quote.

Make reservations well ahead for peak seasons: Carnival (February), Easter and from June to the end of September. If you arrive on spec, try the hotel booking offices at the airport and the railway station.

Deluxe Hotels
For a double room with a bath expect to pay L400,000–L700,00 and over per night.

CIPRIANI
Giudecca 10.
Tel: 520 7744.
On the island of Giudecca with pri-

vate launch to run you to San Marco. The ultimate in luxury with 98 lavish rooms, luxuriant gardens, Olympic-size pool (the only private one in central Venice), tennis and a fully equipped fitness centre. The annexe, the Palazzo Vendramin, is a 15th-century *palazzo* with nine luxury suites, provided with kitchenette, marble bathroom and whirlpool. Closed winter.

HOTEL DANIELI
Riva degli Schiavoni, Castello 4196.
Tel: 522 6480.
Two hundred and thirty-eight rooms. Old Gothic palazzo with superb views across the lagoon. Doge Dandolo used to live here; Dickens, Wagner, Ruskin, Balzac are among the names on the guest list. Lobby has neo-Byzantine splendour, bedrooms are mainly in Venetian baroque style. Wonderful views from rooftop restaurant. Pity about the graceless 1950s extension.

GRITTI PALACE
Campo S Maria del Giglio,
San Marco 2467.
Tel: 794611.
Eighty eight rooms, former private *palazzo* of Doge Andrea Gritti overlooking Grand Canal. Room 10 is where Hemingway stayed. Generally agreed to be the most exclusive hotel in Venice.

Expensive Hotels
Count on L180,000–L400,000 for a double room with bath.

LONDRA PALACE
Riva degli Schiavoni, Castello 4171
Tel: 520 0533
Sixty nine rooms and '100 windows overlooking the lagoon'. A comfortable and civilised hotel with club-style bar, French restaurant and afternoon teas.

MONACO & GRAND HOTEL
Calle Vallaresso, San Marco 1325.
Tel: 520 0211.
Seventy five rooms, exceptional setting on Grand Canal with splendid views. A hotel of much charm and character which feels more intimate than it really is.

SATURNIA & INTERNATIONAL
Calle Larga XXII Marzo,
San Marco 2398.
Tel: 520 8377.
Ninety five rooms, in an old *palazzo* owned by a family of doges; set on a smart shopping street close to Piazza San Marco. Two restaurants, one of which is open-air.

Moderate Hotels
L85,000–L210,000 for a double room with bath.

ACCADEMIA VILLA MARAVEGE
Fondamenta Bollani,
Dorsoduro 1058–60.
Tel: 521 0188.
Twenty seven rooms. No longer the bargain it used to be, but still very desirable for its quiet location (close to the Accademia gallery) and homely atmosphere. Reservations required well in advance.

DO POZZI
Calle Larga XXII Marzo,
S Marco 2373.
Tel: 520 7855.
Twenty nine rooms, small and spruce hotel in quiet cul-de-sac conveniently close to Piazza San Marco. The adjoining restaurant, the Raffaele, has canal-side tables.

LA FENICE ET DES ARTISTES
Campiello de la Fenice,
San Marco 1936.
Tel: 523 2333.
Sixty five rooms, many of which are taken by performers at the neighbouring Fenice opera house; good value for Venice, with plenty of charm and character.

FLORA
Calle Larga XXII Marzo,
San Marco 2283A.
Tel: 520 5844.
Forty four rooms. One of the most desirable small hotels in Venice with quiet garden, pretty décor and location close to Piazza San Marco.

SAN MOISÉ
San Marco 2058.
Tel: 520 3755.
Sixteen rooms, on canal near the Fenice opera house. Small, friendly and quiet with traditional Venetian style fabrics and furnishings. Very

convenient for Piazza San Marco. All rooms have TV and minibar.

Inexpensive Hotels and Pensions
Inexpensive by Venetian standards means L70,000–L100,000 for a double room.

ABBAZIA
Calle Priuli, Cannaregio 66–8.
Tel: 717333.
Thirty six rooms. Converted monastery with garden. Useful if you need to stay within easy reach of Piazzale Roma or the station.

AGLI ALBORETTI
Rio Terrà Sant'Agnese,
Dorsoduro 882–4.
Tel: 523 0058.
Nineteen rooms. Simple and homely, close to Accademia gallery.

BUCINTORO
Riva degli Schiavoni, Castello 2135.
Tel: 522 3240.
Twenty eight rooms. Good-value, friendly *pensione* right on the waterfront near the Arsenale. Simple rooms, many with splendid views of the lagoon. Four floors but no lift. Halfboard terms available.

CALCINA
Zattere, Dorsoduro 780.
Tel: 520 6466.
Thirty seven rooms, many looking across to the island of Giudecca. Setting compensates for dowdy décor. Ruskin stayed here.

GALLERIA
Accademia 878A.
Tel: 520 4172.
Part of a 17th-century *palazzo* facing the Grand Canal, just a stone's throw away from the Accademia gallery. Very good value in comparison to rooms in San Marco.

Four-star hotel across the road from the beach. Best known as the setting for the book and film of *Death in Venice* and still has an air of grandeur. Large gardens, pool, tennis courts and private cabins – at a price – on the beach.

Hotel Excelsior
Lungomare Marconi 41.
Tel: 526 0201.
Two hundred and eighteen rooms. Five-star, big, modernised hotel by the beach close to casino with gardens, pool and tennis courts.

Villa Ada
Via E Dandolo, 24.
Tel: 526 0120.
A far cheaper alternative to the above. Three turn-of-the-century villas a few minutes from the beach which you can reach on complimentary bikes.

La Residenza
Campo Bandiera e Moro,
Castello 3608.
Tel: 528 5315.
Seventeen rooms, in handsome 15th-century Venetian Gothic *palazzo* overlooking small square a stone's throw from the Riva degli Schiavoni. Quiet, inconspicuous as a hotel – very much appeals to the independent traveller.

San Fantin
Campiello Fenice, San Marco 1930A.
Tel: 523 1401.
Fourteen rooms. Simple, homely and very handy for the Fenice opera house.

Seguso
Zattere, Dorsoduro 779.
Tel: 528 6858.
Thirty six rooms. *Pensione* which appeals, particularly to the British and French, for its charm and splendid views across to Giudecca. Half-board terms available.

Hotels on the Lido
All the following are closed in winter.

Hotel Des Bains
Lungomare Marconi 17.
Tel: 526 5921.
One hundred and ninety-five rooms.

TOURIST INFORMATION

The most central office for tourist information is the Azienda di Promozione Turistica at Piazza San Marco 71C, under the arch just west of the square (Tel: 522 6356). Their opening hours are unpredictable. You can pick up a reasonably good map of the city here and a current list of opening hours – though only on request. Ask too for a copy of *Un Ospite di Venezia*, an indispensable booklet in Italian and English, giving a wide range of practical information such as current listings, waterbus routes and charges for all types of transport. It comes out every other Monday and runs out

tion, restaurants, museums shops, excursions, etc. The card, available from the main tourist offices at the railway station and 71C Piazza San Marco, is free of charge, but you must take a photograph and passport or ID card.

Pensioners

For the over 60s (on presentation of passport/ID card) the Accademia gallery and the Ca d'Oro are free of charge.

FURTHER READING

The list of books on Venice is endless. Many of them are out of print but you should have no difficulty in finding those recommended below.

Guidebooks

Honour, Hugh, *The Companion Guide to Venice*. 1965 and 1977. Definitely one of the most readable, informative and enjoyable books on Venice.

Kent, John, *Venice – A Colour Guide to the City,* Viking 1988. Beautifully illustrated guide, identifying 475 buildings of Venice. Short, lively text, full of amusing anecdote.

Links, J G, *Venice for Pleasure*, The Bodley Head, revised 1984. Delightful guide to walks in Venice, punctuated with plenty of coffee stops.

Lorenzetti, Giulio, *Venice and its Lagoon* (translated by John Guthrie). The authoritative guide for the really serious student. Extraordinarily de-

fast. There are other branches of the APT at the station (Tel: 719078) the Lido (Gran Viale) and, if you are coming by car, Rotonda Marghera, at the end of the highway by the AGIP petrol station. Hotel reservations however can only be made at the station and at Rotonda Marghera.

For information by post write to the Azienda di Promozione Turistica di Venezia, Castello 4421.

The phone number for information and advice in English (and other languages) is 111.

SPECIAL SERVICES

Disabled Visitors

Consult the useful *Veneziapertutti* (Venice for all) map which highlights all the accessible areas and shows that 42 per cent of the interesting buildings can be reached without crossing a single bridge. It also lists hotels which are suitable for the disabled. Available from ULSS, Dorsoduro 3493, free of charge.

Youth Passes

Anyone under 29 is entitled to a Youth Pass or *Carta Giovani*, which gives discount rates on accommoda-

tailed and informative. Pity about the index. Hard to get outside Venice.

History
Hibbert, Christopher, *Venice – The Biography of a City*, Grafton Books 1988, reprinted 1989. A superb survey of Venice, highly readable and informative; a combination of history, narrative and guidebook.

Lauritzen, Peter, *Venice – A Thousand Years of Culture and Civilization (the story of Venice)*, Atheneum, New York 1978.
Morris, Jan, *A Sea Voyage*. Voyage along the historic Venetian trade routes wandering from past to present. A lucid history of the empire.
Norwich, John Julius, *A History of Venice*, Penguin 1983. Detailed, well written history up to the end of the republic, regarded as the standard work of Venetian history in English.

Art and Architecture
Liberman, Ralph, *Renaissance Architecture in Venice, 1450–1540*. Frederick Muller Ltd, London, 1982. Venetian architecture from florid late Gothic to High Renaissance.
Ruskin, John, *The Stones of Venice*, 1853. Classic account of the buildings of Venice, for the serious lover of architecture. The abridged version (edited by J G Links) puts the original – nearly half a million words – within reach of travellers with limited time.
Steer, John, *Venetian Painting*, Thames & Hudson's 'World of Art' series. Well-illustrated and scholarly guide to the Venetian school.

Novels
Hemingway, Ernest, *Across the River and into the Trees*, Panther 1977 (originally published 1950).
James, Henry, *The Aspern Papers*, Penguin, 1988.
Mann, Thomas, *Death in Venice*, Penguin 1971 (originally published in 1921).
Proust, Marcel, *Albertine Disparue*, 1925 (part of *A la Recherche du Temps Perdu* and translated into English as *The Sweet Cheat Gone* – originally published 1925).

Others
James, Henry, *Italian Hours*, Century 1988 (originally published 1909). Includes 5 essays on Venice in the 1860s and 1970s.
McCarthy, Mary, *Venice Preserved*, New York, Reynal, 1956.
Morris, Jan, *Venice*. Faber, revised edition 1983. Brilliantly witty account of the city, a must.
Norwich, John Julius (ed), *Venice, a Travellers' Companion*, Constable, London.

WHEN THE CHOICE IS ITALY, IT'S CITALIA FOR CHOICE

BEACHES

ISLANDS

LAKES

MOUNTAINS

CITIES

TWO AND THREE CENTRES

HOLIDAYS BY OUR OWN TRAIN

COACH TOURS

VENICE SIMPLON-ORIENT-EXPRESS

COUNTRY VILLAS AND APARTMENTS

MOTORING HOLIDAYS

INDEPENDENT TRAVEL ARRANGEMENTS

STAY AND CRUISE

FLY DRIVE

SKIING HOLIDAYS

Citalia

MARCO POLO HOUSE, 3-5 LANSDOWNE ROAD, CROYDON CR9 1LL.
CITALIA SALES: 081-686 5533   TAILOR MADE: 081-688 9989
ATOL 285BCD CIT (ENGLAND) ABTA 17764

Index

Art & Photo Credits

Photography	**Chris Donaghue** *and*
1, 4, 11, 77т, 78, 79	**Lyle Lawson**
10, 15, 44	**Archive for Kunst und Geschichte, Berlin**
16, 54	**Benjamin Legde**
32т	**Günter Schneider**
Publisher	**Hans Höfer**
Design Concept	**V Barl**
Designer	**Gareth Walters**
Cover Design	**Klaus Geisler**
Editor	**Chris Catling**
Managing Editor	**Andrew Eames**
Cartography	**Berndtson & Berndtson**

INSIGHT GUIDES

COLORSET NUMBERS

You'll find the colorset number on the spine of each Insight Guide.

INSIGHT *pocket* GUIDES

• •

United States: **Houghton Mifflin Company, Boston MA 02108**
Tel: (800) 2253362 Fax: (800) 4589501

Canada: **Thomas Allen & Son, 390 Steelcase Road East**
Markham, Ontario L3R 1G2
Tel: (416) 4759126 Fax: (416) 4756747

Great Britain: **GeoCenter UK, Hampshire RG22 4BJ**
Tel: (256) 817987 Fax: (256) 817988

Worldwide: **Höfer Communications Singapore 2262**
Tel: (65) 8612755 Fax: (65) 8616438

66 I was first drawn to the Insight Guides by the excellent "Nepal" volume. I can think of no book which so effectively captures the essence of a country. Out of these pages leaped the Nepal I know – the captivating charm of a people and their culture. I've since discovered and enjoyed the entire Insight Guide Series. Each volume deals with a country or city in the same sensitive depth, which is nowhere more evident than in the superb photography. **99**

Sir Edmund Hillary